Danger UXB

M. J. Jappy is a freelance television producer who has specialized in factual and lifestyle programming over the last nine years. As well as *Danger UXB*, she has worked on *Secret History: The Roswell Incident* and *If You Can't Stand the Heat*. She has recently completed a six-month sabbatical in Bali where she has written her first novel.

DO's AND DONT's FOR BOMB DISPOSAL.

DO TAKE EVERY SAFETY PRECAUTION

DONT TAKE ANY UNNECESSARY RISKS.

DO REPORT ANYTHING STRANGE TO I.O.F. & D.B.D. (TEL. ABB. 2315) WHERE THE I.O. WILL SUPPLY ADVICE AND ASSISTANCE.

DONT TALK ABOUT YOUR EXPLOITS. IT MAY HELP THE ENEMY TO CHANGE HIS METHODS.

DO, WHEN WORKING ON A ⑰ FUZE, LISTEN AT FREQUENT INTERVALS (SAY 5 MINS) TO THE CLOCK.

DO READ AND DIGEST THE INTELLIGENCE SUMMARIES. THE INFORMATION MAY BE OF THE GREATEST USE TO YOU.

DONT LEAVE TOOLS AND PLANT LYING ABOUT OR THEY WILL BE MISSING NEXT TIME THEY ARE WANTED.

· **DO** REMEMBER THAT IT IS YOUR DUTY TO INSPIRE CONFIDENCE, SO DO NOT TRY TO IMPRESS BY "TELLING THE TALE".

DONT TRY TO TAKE ANYTHING TO PIECES UNLESS YOU KNOW EXACTLY WHAT YOU ARE TRYING TO DO.

DONT ALLOW ANYONE BUT THE DRIVER ON A VEHICLE CARRYING A LIVE BOMB.

DONT FORGET - THAT THOUGH YOUR WORK IS INEVITABLY DIRTY - SMARTNESS COUNTS.

DO RESPECT PRIVATE PROPERTY - A BOMBED HOUSE IS STILL SOMEBODY'S HOME.

DONT COLLECT SOUVENIRS.

DO KEEP TOOLS & PLANT IN GOOD WORKING ORDER.

DONT LEAVE ESSENTIAL TOOLS AND STORES BEHIND.

DO KEEP ON CORDIAL TERMS WITH THE LOCAL CIVIL AUTHORITIES

AND REMEMBER ALWAYS THAT YOU BELONG TO THE CORPS OF

ROYAL ENGINEERS

Danger UXB

The Remarkable Story of the Disposal of
Unexploded Bombs during the Second World War

M. J. JAPPY

For my father, who might have liked this book.

First published in 2001 by Channel 4 Books

This edition published 2003 by Channel 4 Books
an imprint of Pan Macmillan Ltd
Pan Macmillan, 20 New Wharf Road, London, N1 9RR
Associated comanies throughout the world
www.panmacmillan.com

ISBN 0 7522 1576 0

1 3 5 7 9 8 6 4 2

A CIP catalogue record for this book is available
from the British Library

Design, reproduction and typesetting by Production Line
Printed by Mackays of Chatham plc

Contents

Acknowledgements

THE GREATEST SHARE OF GRATITUDE must go to those who told their stories. The films could not have been made without the help and generosity of all the contributors, whose testimony forms a large and crucial part of the text of this book. The willingness with which they gave up both their time and their memories was overwhelming. Meeting each and every one of them was enlightening for all the team involved, taking us on a fascinating journey. In this regard my heartfelt thanks and affection go out to Ernest Acton, Stuart Archer, Montague 'Ferdy' Bool, Richard Bridge, Cecil Brinton, Peter Chamberlain, Jack Curtis, John Hannaford, Frank Henry, Professor John Hudson, Jimmy Melrose, Lionel Meynell, Nicho Poland, Ken Revis, Bryan Richards, Sir John Rowlands, Dr Raymond Sharp, Harry Vallance, Eric Wakeling, Bert Woolhouse, Bill Wooton and Christopher Wren.

I would also like to thank Arthur Hogben, Pat Beaumont, Jill Buch, Joyce Farthing, Bill Filer, Julian Malec, Hannah Kennard and the *Grimsby Evening Telegraph*, John Wilson and Carol Moss at the North East Lincolnshire Archive, Felicity Goodall, Ted Hill at the HMS *Belfast* Association, Diana Harrison, the Earl of Suffolk and Berkshire, Reg Journet at the Royal Engineers Association, the family of the late Lieutenant Commander John Ouvry, and the Imperial War Museum in London and Duxford.

The two-part documentary film on which this book is based was the brainchild of its director and producer Geoffrey Smith, and it is to him that this book owes its genesis. His enthusiasm brought me 11,000 miles to work with him and his dedication to his craft was infectious. Huge thanks are similarly owed to Lore Windemuth, my co-conspirator in occasional 'director' management and provider of all the research on the German side of the story. Thanks must also be heaped upon Martin Smith whose support and encouragement were often sought and always valued. I would also like to thank the 'X' men, Mike Fox, Mike Lax and Chris Cox, whose sensitivity and interest in the subject took them far beyond what was expected of a 'normal' crew and helped bring Geoffrey's vision to the screen and these pages. In a similar vein, thanks must also be extended to Paul Nathan whose superlative boom-handling will be long remembered. Our production manager Deborah McTaggart, whose help is also appreciated, ably managed a demanding schedule throughout and was particularly helpful co-ordinating the stills needed for the book. Thanks must also go to Isabel de Bertodano, without whom much of the primary source material would not have been found in time.

I also thank my copy editor, Christine King, and my agent, Luigi Bonomi, for their unending patience and support through an extremely tight schedule.

Foreword

YEARS AFTER EVERYONE ELSE had read Michael Ondaatje's novel *The English Patient*, I found myself with a copy of it on holiday. The book took me to the strange isolation of a crumbling Italian villa near the end of the war, where the main characters inhabited a world none of them seemed to have much control over. Kip, the Sikh bomb disposal sapper, struck me as different, however. Playing around with bombs had forced him to have a sense of calm and, strangely, given that bombs are so unpredictable, a surety about the world and his place in it. I liked him, and when I read in the footnotes that Ondaatje had used the real-life account of a bomb disposal officer for his research, I just had to find out more.

During several rewarding afternoons at the British Library, I grew more fascinated with the world of bomb disposal. Men down 10-metre holes, knee deep in mud or water, defuzing 1,000 kilograms of steel and TNT with just a few crude tools. Unsure of what fuze or booby-trap each new bomb contained, many of the men who started the job in 1940 didn't survive beyond ten weeks.

I pictured all the movie clichés of clocks ticking down to zero and people sweating over which wire to cut, and realized they paled against the drama and suspense of what these men had been through. As one author and bomb disposal officer, Major A. B. Hartley, said, '1940 was the heroic age of bomb disposal, a period of individual prowess when urgency and a lack of knowledge and equipment led to the taking of fantastic risks, to fantastic escapes and to many many deaths.'

All this was gripping stuff, but would anyone still be alive to talk to? Well, one thing led to another and before long I had several names and addresses. I spent hours with these wonderful men, and was struck by their youthfulness, humour and humility. Is taking risks every day for years on end the elixir of life? It would seem to be so.

But although I learnt a great deal from them, they were all unable to share in my intense curiosity about what they had done. 'It was just a job, and we had to get on and do it,' they kept saying. My generation doesn't readily understand the concept of selfless duty, so I was left trying to imagine what it was like to go down one of those deep shafts and do battle with a huge, silent killer. It was a vain task and I realized that the only way of answering my questions about bomb disposal was to make a film about these men's experiences.

I hope both this book and the television series it accompanies will take you on a similar journey to the one all of us involved with their production have made. It was a rather obscure road at times, particularly when we tried to discover what the German fuze designers were doing and thinking, but I have now been down a shaft with a bomb, albeit a dead one, and have also had the great pleasure and privilege of meeting and working with some lovely people. Thank you to all the bomb disposal officers and men who so gladly participated in the film and to those of their number who fought so bravely against a very different sort of enemy.

GEOFFREY SMITH
SERIES PRODUCER AND DIRECTOR

Introduction

'There has been an awful lot of bad news on this course, sir. Do you have anything "good" to tell us?'

'Yes, I do as it happens. The medical boffins have discovered that when a bomb goes off, it explodes faster than the human nervous system can react. In short, you won't feel a thing.'

STORY TOLD BY JOHN HANNAFORD

TO MANY PEOPLE THESE DAYS, the idea of 'bomb disposal' conjures up images shaped principally by television and – more colourfully – cinema. Perhaps the empty streets of a threatened town lie unnaturally quiet. Doors of hurriedly abandoned houses may swing and bang in the wind. Zoom in on one brave soldier, weighed down with hi-tech equipment and lumbering in heavy body armour (or, of course, a secret agent or detective hero without any visible means of tackling the bomb). Tension mounts as he identifies the device, which often – and conveniently – shows an illuminated countdown to doom. Minutes, then seconds, tick agonizingly away. At last (and it usually is at the last moment), he cuts the correct wire and another armageddon is averted.

Entertaining drama, no doubt – but usually bearing little resemblance to the actual world of bomb disposal. A real flesh and blood soldier faces a device that may have no markings to indicate what kind of detonator is employed or what mechanism will set it off. These are devious weapons and this isn't the movies. There is no clock counting down to zero hour, and certainly no happy guesswork. And Hollywood's dramatic scenarios crank up the tension to a pitch that would be counter-productive in real-life situations. What is genuine, though, is the ever-present danger: not for nothing is the distance from the bomb to the nearest safe point called 'the longest walk'.

Modern technology has brought great advances in methods of detecting bombs and making them safe, and indeed failure for today's bomb disposal officers is a comparatively rare occurrence. Yet statistically, bomb disposal is still one of the most dangerous areas of operation in the armed services – as it always has been. In military terms, explosive ordnance disposal (as it has come to be known today) has a very short history, essentially dating to the last century – and, most significantly, the Second World War.

The Luftwaffe dropped over half a million bombs on Britain from 1939 to 1945. The bomb disposal units of the three armed services dealt with over 45,000 that did not explode, a figure that does not include the tens of thousands of anti-personnel devices and hundreds of thousands of mines that were still being made safe long after the end of the war. The implications of this figure may seem rather meaningless until you remember the chaos that can be caused in the twenty-first century by just one discarded holdall at a railway station: someone's dirty laundry can literally bring a city to a standstill. Not so for the bomb disposal personnel of the Second World War. The war effort could not be held up for any reason, and if that meant they had to defuze a bomb with a trembler switch next to working railway lines or take away a ticking time bomb on the back of a lorry, then so be it.

The men who did this work stared the enemy in the face for the entire duration of the war, and yet the majority of them never left their native shores. Such was the danger involved that, despite not being the most obviously 'brave' role in the military, in the middle of 1940 the life expectancy of a bomb disposal officer was barely ten weeks.

The blitzes on London and the industrial heartland of Coventry, and the devastation wrought on Clydebank, are clearly remembered by those who survived them. The destruction and the loss of life are well documented and will never be forgotten. But the number of lives that were saved, and the scale of damage prevented, by the sustained courage and devotion to duty of the bomb disposal men is impossible to quantify. And they did their work without any fuss. Indeed, like the work of the Secret Services, their successes could rarely be trumpeted for fear of alerting the enemy to sensitive information: new techniques in defuzing bombs, or the location of undamaged buildings that could be targeted for the next wave of bombing raids. So, ironically, for these men it was in many ways a quiet war: a war without fanfare and where the greatest recognition could amount to a packet of cigarettes from the grateful owner of a house saved from destruction.

A quiet war and a lonely one too, for many of the men. In the Royal Engineers, the Corps that dealt with the majority of bomb disposal work on mainland Britain, the companies were split into sections of a few men and one officer before being dispatched to billets far away from their comrades. Theirs was not the camaraderie of the officers' mess or the NAAFI canteen. A more casual chain of command existed in bomb disposal, with officers and men each valuing the role of the other without the need for pulling rank or mechanically obeying orders. Their uniforms may have been forever caked in mud and their boots unpolished, but it would be impossible to find an officer who would speak ill of his men.

Their achievements are all the more remarkable given the way in which the bomb disposal organization was formed. The first German bombs were dropped on the British Isles in October 1939, and the first to land yet not explode came barely a month later. The more cynical historian may feel it was perhaps a pity that these unexploded bombs landed in the Shetland Islands, at Sullom Voe. Arguably, had they been closer to London, the ill-prepared British government might have been galvanized into taking earlier action.

At this stage there was not one member of the armed services officially designated to deal with them. Preparations regarding bomb-disposal parties amounted to little more than giving half a dozen men two shovels and a pair of picks, and an officer-training programme consisting of a brief rundown on how a British bomb worked. Strange, considering that not many British bombs were dropped by the Germans... Nine months later, the hurriedly formed Bomb Disposal Companies, now strategically placed across the country, dealt with over 2,000 unexploded bombs in the first twenty days of September 1940 alone.

It was very much a question of learning on the job, improvising techniques – and adapting to new and unexpected challenges. There was no question of the enemy sticking to a predictable reper-toire of weapons. At times a deadly game of 'cat and mouse' was played out between German and British technical ingenuity. As soon as the bomb disposal men had worked out how to deal with one type of bomb, it seemed as if a new one arrived to perplex them once more.

As Major John Hudson, a bomb disposal officer who also worked in research, now says, 'Of course, the first thing they needed was a knowledge of the fuzes themselves: how they worked, how they might be recognized and, if possible, made safe. This involved getting samples of these fuzes as soon as possible at whatever risk.'

On the ground, the game of cat and mouse looked more like 'chicken and egg': without the correct equipment it was extremely difficult to remove the fuzes. But without the fuzes with which to experiment, the equipment could never be made. Eric Wakeling was then a young lieutenant, and remembers the dilemma:

We had nothing at all to deal with these fuzes. We didn't know what was going to be in these unexploded bombs, and men and officers were risking their lives to take these fuzes out. When you're dealing with something you know nothing about, you're bound to have accidents – if you can call it an accident.'

Why would anyone want to do this job? Today, within reason, it is possible to choose in which branch of the services one wishes to serve. Of course, this was a luxury open to few who joined up or were conscripted in the war years. The bomb disposal arms of the Royal Air Force, Royal Navy or the Army were not postings of choice for most although, interestingly, over 300 conscientious objectors did volunteer for such work.

Bomb disposal in the Second World War did require certain qualities, which were more complex than being 'unmarried and a good sprinter', as suggested by one young officer. The officers of the Royal Engineers, whose job it was to supervise the uncovering and neutralizing of a bomb, often came from professional backgrounds such as engineering or architecture. The other ranks, or sappers as they are known, often had a trade such as carpentry, joinery or, even more usefully, mining and tunnelling. The mental attributes needed were much harder to pinpoint. It must be remembered that this was an era before psychometric testing and a time when, had it even been available, the luxury of being able to discard an otherwise fit individual on psychological grounds was one that the recruiting offices could hardly afford. It will never be known how many of the hundreds of soldiers killed in this line of work were unlucky or just manifestly unsuited to the job. To many people, such an analysis of a time when making the best of it was the best that could be done is both unnecessary and irrelevant. However, certain evaluations can be made.

Those who survived to tell their stories speak of being 'temperamentally suited' to the job. Lionel Meynell was one of the first officers to be moved into bomb disposal from a field company of the Royal Engineers; he recalls:

It wasn't an insurmountable job. I do think that there were officers who were posted to bomb disposal companies who were rather incapable of ever conquering the fear that the bomb might go off. I never treated any bomb with contempt. I was

always conscious of mentally going through every single thing
there was to do. I think that one or two people might have been
killed through being careless.

To those of us who will never be in the position to share their experiences, it is impossible to know how we would react. Can you imagine what it would be like to dig down through the concrete of a factory floor, never knowing if the bomb beneath your feet was going to go off at any second? What would it really be like to lie flat on your stomach in muddy water at the bottom of a 10-metre-deep shaft, the sides of which could cave in at any time? What does 1,000 kilograms of steel and TNT feel like as you run your hands underneath it to feel if it has one or two fuze pockets, all the time knowing that if you felt the second, the slightest touch could cause it to explode? Would you wonder why your life was less precious than the machine tools being made in the factory above? Could you really believe it was 'just a job', as the men themselves always claimed?

Heroics were not an option. Some of the saddest stories are of life lost through a moment's distraction or foolhardiness; a desire to get home quickly, have the latest 'souvenir' or take a shortcut in a job where the long way round was almost always preferable. But there are also stories of immense courage and immense good fortune. Indeed, some of the greatest breakthroughs in the war against unexploded bombs emerged from the luck of a very few people. Possibly the right people in the right places at the right times.

The men who worked in bomb disposal and survived do not think of themselves as being special. Even today, their heroism passes them by. Their story has never truly been explored before because many of those who survived find it is hard to put into words. As retired lieutenant John Hannaford says:

It's very difficult for people to understand what it's like to be
down a hole, a deep hole with a cold, sinister-looking steel
bomb. One minute you are there and the next there's oblivion.

To this day I've never talked about it. I don't know the reason for it, even my brother officers, when we meet, we never talk about what we did in the war – never, never, never. I don't know why, but we don't. We were on our own and to this day we are still on our own.

The aim of this book is to give a voice to those men who survived, and to echo that of the men who did not.

1

Pass the buck – there's a war on...

Bomb disposal sections were just formed overnight and sent out to do a job. You didn't know what you were going to get or what you were going to meet. It was no wonder that the life expectancy of a subaltern in those days was about ten weeks.

COLONEL ERIC WAKELING RE

IN 1939 MOST PEOPLE would have shrugged their shoulders if asked to explain the acronym UXB. At that time it would have sounded more like a brand of washing soda than the convenient handle yet to be given to the tens of thousands of bombs that failed to explode during the Second World War. The phrase 'Danger UXB', scrawled in red paint on to a sign swinging from a gate, daubed on the door of a newly destroyed house or strung across the end of guarded road, was to become one of the most evocative signs of wartime. For millions of people, in both town and countryside, the sign became part of the vernacular of Britain at war.

An unexploded bomb was not only dangerous: it was also a disruptive force. Arguably, a UXB in one place, which was not dealt with quickly, caused more problems than a bomb dropped somewhere else that did explode. Initially, it had been broadly assumed that a bomb, when dropped, either exploded or it did not. A few people had given thought to the implications of dealing with a TNT-packed steel case still fitted with a fuze, but such a question was not at the top of the agenda for a government occupied with how far Hitler's march across Europe would take him. From records of the time, it would appear that the country was ill-prepared for the magnitude of the problem it was about to face. To understand why, it is important to examine the political chaos out of which the bomb disposal organization was born.

Although the scale of bombing on mainland Britain was certainly not anticipated, aerial bombardment was by no means a new phenomenon: zeppelins such as the *Hindenburg* had dropped bombs on London in small numbers during the First World War, and shells were also used widely with devastating effect on the battlefields of France and Belgium. By the late 1930s, Europe was yet again on the brink of global conflict. In contravention of the 1919 Treaty of Versailles, Germany had been rearming itself for many years, and had supplied aerial support to the Franco regime in Spain. By 1939 there had been significant progress in the use of aerial bombardment as an effective means of prosecuting war. Indeed, if the British government were in any doubt about Germany's confidence in mounting a successful air war they need have looked no further than the reports coming back from Spain.

The German war machine had been using bombs extensively against both civilians and troops in the Spanish Civil War. General Franco had been more than happy to let the Luftwaffe use his countrymen for target practice, and Herman Goering, who commanded the Luftwaffe, had many opportunities to obtain detailed information on the effectiveness of the German bombing strategy. Its success was apparent in the destruction of many cities, and stories of the unfolding human disaster were well covered in the British press. But to many people in Britain, another war with Germany – only twenty years after 'the war to end all wars' – was almost impossible to imagine. Furthermore, even if that leap of imagination had taken place, there would still have been little understanding of the effect of bombardment. Today, we have television to convey with awful immediacy and vividness the destruction wrought by warfare, but in the 1930s most people could not have envisaged the devastation caused by just one bomb in an urban area.

However, the warnings were there. One government agent's report that found its way back from Spain said:

If there is one lesson beyond all others that the English people should learn from the Spanish Civil War and the part played in that struggle by Germany and Italy, it is the importance attached by the air forces of both of these powers to the undermining of civilian morale by aircraft attacks on cities... Although little is heard of it in the world press, owing to the fact that there are few correspondents in Valencian territory, hardly a day passes without the bombing of such places as Tarragona, Castellon, Sagunto, Valencia, Cartagena, Almeria and even Barcelona, and there is no doubt that these attacks are affecting the morale of the civilian populations.

Yet several months into the Second World War there was still a confidence bordering on arrogance supporting the belief that Germany would not bomb British civilians. One young man from the ranks of the Royal Engineers remembers the reception he received at the hands of one senior officer. Sapper Ernest Acton and his section were attached to the 2nd Battalion of the Cheshire Regiment at Endcliffe Hall in Sheffield. As soon as the battalion's major saw their uniforms, they were dispatched to draw up a schedule of lessons to teach the men about wiring, digging and all the other tasks with which the Royal Engineers were normally associated. Sapper Acton was quick to point out that the reason they were in Sheffield was not to train apprentice electricians. The reaction from the major illustrated that there was a substantial amount of complacency in the upper ranks still to be swept away, as Acton recalls:

'I'm sorry, sir,' I said, 'but we're a bomb disposal section.'
He said, 'What's that?'

I told him we were here to deal with enemy bombs. He said, 'Good God, man! Who's going to drop bombs on this country!' This was before Dunkirk, of course. We hadn't had that terrible tragedy, so things seemed rosy. [The major] couldn't see German aeroplanes coming here. He hadn't given it a thought.

Should the government have anticipated the immense problem that UXBs were to become? Air raids were certainly foreseen. As early as 1924, a report by the Air Staff had predicted that there would be 11.5 deaths per thousand tonnes of explosives dropped: 1,700 would be killed in the first twenty-four hours, 1,275 in the second and 850 every day following. The conclusion was that anarchy would quickly follow. The government's solution had been to start digging bunkers to protect against bombs: by 1933 it had created an underground haven for the Treasury in Storey's Gate protected by 17 feet (5 metres) of concrete and iron bars, consisting of 200 rooms in 600 acres of office space. In addition there were three subterranean citadels in the London suburbs: the Admiralty was to be based at Cricklewood (Margaret Thatcher was to use this bunker during the Falklands War in 1981) and the Air Ministry at Harrow, while the codenamed 'Paddock' was to be the Cabinet's HQ situated beneath the Post Office Research Station at nearby Dollis Hill in north-west London.

While the government was busy creating shelters for its departments, it was not affording such protection to the public. They had to make do with a booklet published in 1938: *The Protection of Your Home Against Air Raid*. This pamphlet provided very useful information about the evacuation of pets but sadly failed to mention any of the basics one might need to excavate oneself or one's family from under a pile of rubble.

In any case there was a greater fear than airborne bombing. The memory of it had lingered since the First World War: gas.

The horrors of the gas that filled the trenches of the First World War had all but obliterated the home front's recollections of bombing by the *Hindenburg* and other 'Hun' aircraft on mainland Britain. Memories of the craters left by shells and the 1,414 recorded deaths had faded along with the scars of over 3,000 people injured by bombing in London. In the meantime, however, London County Council had been preparing for gas attacks for many years. By the mid 1930s Lincoln's Inn Fields housed a trench network 7 feet (just over 2 metres) deep and 1,430 feet (436 metres) long. It was covered with concrete and 2 feet (60 centimetres) of topsoil, and air locks were fitted to the entrances to stop the gas penetrating. Similar trenches were dug around London, including in such squares as Bloomsbury, Russell and Woburn. The government bunkers were also constructed to protect against gas attack.

By the time war was declared on 3 September 1939, there were hundreds of men ready to be mobilized to combat the effects of a gas attack. They were organized into three companies each comprising three sections. Each section had ample equipment, and the men's training had been extensive and detailed. On the home front, every man, woman and child was given a gas mask, which was to be taken everywhere day and night. Eric Wakeling, who went on to become a bomb disposal officer, started his career in Number 59 Company, Royal Engineers, a chemical warfare company. He was to find a sharp contrast between the two areas of operations.

The [government] embarked on a massive campaign to produce as many chemical warfare companies as possible in the shortest possible time. They opened up their first one, Number 11 Chemical Warfare Training Battalion, at Winterbourne near to Porton, the research establishment. Two companies were formed, mainly from Territorial Army units in South Wales, and all of them went out to France in early January 1940. I was on the draft and was pulled out because I was going to get my commission. Then I went to another chemical warfare company in the second group and was absolutely amazed at the amount of equipment they had. There were three sections in a company; each had a motorbike, a pick-up truck, a utility vehicle, twelve or thirteen 15-hundredweight trucks and I think two or three

30-hundredweight trucks. That was one section! There were three of them in a company, plus company headquarters vehicles, all brand new, straight from the factory.

Compare this largesse with the minimal resources allotted to those who came to deal with unexploded bombs as far on as July 1940. What had led to such a disparity and why, when gas was never used in Britain but unexploded bombs went on to cause chaos and disruption on a massive scale, was the government not better prepared?

It would seem that it comes down to a confluence of several factors. There was reluctance to accept responsibility at a time when priorities were extremely difficult to determine. Each government department was unwilling to leave itself burdened with a job that would add unduly to its workload. And, of course, we have seen that many people were unable to contemplate bombs being dropped in the first place, let alone what happened to those that failed to explode. However, just as the threat of airborne attack had been recognized by a few percipient people, so some others were aware of the possible problem of UXBs. Warnings were being made as early as 1938 that preparations were nowhere near adequate.

Up until late 1938 it was decreed that the police should 'report all cases of unexploded bombs to the nearest Military Authority, who will arrange for disposal of them'. But by 5 November of that year, the War Office sought to off-load its responsibility to the Home Office by suggesting that the present arrangements were inadequate. A War Office communication to the Under Secretary of State at the Home Office read:

I am commanded by the Army Council to refer to the subject of the disposal of unexploded enemy bombs dropped in the UK in time of war and to say for the information of Secretary, Sir Samuel Hoare, that the Council have had this matter under consideration and after consultation with the Air Ministry are not satisfied that the existing arrangements in this respect are adequate...

I am to say that the Council consider that though these arrangements were adequate under the conditions of the last War, they would be totally inadequate to deal with the quantity of unexploded bombs which might be expected under present circumstances, and they further are of the opinion that this service could be undertaken by the Home Office, ARP [Air Raid Precautions] Department, for the following reasons:

(i) The army have not normally got personnel with a knowledge of air bombs likely to be used by the enemy and those that are available are insufficient in numbers and distribution.

(ii) It is understood that the Air Ministry will not be able to undertake this service.

(iii) The Home Office can call on the services of sufficient persons trained in explosives to perform the required duties and who are normally distributed over the country.

I am, therefore, to state that the Council desire that the matter should be re-opened and suggest that a conference of the 'Services Departments' of the Home Office be summoned at an early date to consider the following motions:

(a) That the disposal of unexploded air bombs and anti-aircraft shells in the UK in time of war will be the responsibility of the Home Office.

(b) That the Admiralty, War Office and Air Ministry will co-operate as far as may be necessary in the training of the necessary personnel for this service.

So someone at the War Office was paying attention to the information filtering back from Spain. Reports of the effectiveness of the Luftwaffe's bombing strategy had noted that up to 10 per cent of its bombs failed to explode, with subsequent fear and disruption on the ground. But the issue now was not to try to estimate the prospective scale of the problem, but to try to establish it as someone else's responsibility. The War Office was under increasing pressure, and finding personnel to deal with unexploded bombs was one difficulty they could do without. In the short term, the War Office's gamesmanship seemed to pay off and the ARP officers who were currently in charge of this task remained in charge. Needless to say, the Chief Inspector of Explosives for the Home Office was not at all happy about the situation.

ARP officers had been given vague instructions about sandbagging and contacting the police to arrange for removal of the bombs – which, it seemed, would land like rabbits killed on the road, lying conveniently in open spaces, on the surface, ready to be loaded on to the back of a lorry. The arguments carried on throughout 1939, with memos being shuttled up and down Whitehall on almost a weekly basis. It was not even made clear whether the ARP should really attempt to move the bombs or blow them up in situ. In order to settle the issue once and for all, the government decided to do the only thing possible and have another meeting.

On 15 May 1939 delegates from the War Office, Home Office and Air Ministry met at Horseferry Road in London. Once again, discussions took on their characteristic circular pattern: the War Office wanted the ARP to continue being responsible; the Home Office said the work did not fall within the remit of the ARP; and the Air Ministry were adamant they did not have nearly enough personnel. The only solution was to have more meetings. In the meantime, the responsibility would remain with the Home Office – but the military, which came under the control of the War Office, would undertake to train the men as and when required.

The consensus was that a specially formed force would be necessary and that veteran soldiers could be recruited from the British Legion. The War Office had other ideas, however. They felt that the ARP could still provide the personnel, whom they would train for one day and then send out on their normal duties, defuzing bombs as they appeared. If they found a bomb in a situation that the one-day course did not cover, for example if it were buried, then the Air Ministry would supply back-up. As far as possible, however, all bombs should be sandbagged and exploded where they were.

By November 1939 the War Office had arranged for bomb disposal parties to be formed. They were few in number and comprised one junior non-commissioned officer and two junior ranks. They were supposed to be kitted out with a vehicle, about 30 kilos of explosives, a couple of shovels and several hundred sandbags. If they were lucky they were given equipment to lift the bomb out of its hole in the form of sheer legs (three metal legs that were positioned over the bomb shaft, and on which a pulley could be mounted). Their instructions were minimal and, with the expected raids failing to materialize at the end of 1939 and into 1940, they tended to be forgotten.

Nevertheless, the arguments still raged between the ARP, the Home Office and the War Office. The ARP was extremely anxious that there were no adequate arrangements being made for dealing with bombs in civilian areas. The delay was blamed on a lack of information filtering out from the embryonic research departments which had been studying the bombs that had fallen in Shetland in November 1939. It was felt that there was no point in giving out information regarding defuzing and evacuation until the research was completed. There were, however, signs that the issue was being taken more seriously and after much discussion the Ministry of Home Security issued a circular on 11 May 1940 that laid out the parameters for bomb disposal.

The government had made the decision to split bomb disposal work between the Army, Air Force and Navy. There was significant cross-over – each of the services often supporting one another, pooling information – but broadly speaking, the RAF was responsible for bombs that fell on airfields and that were in crashed aircraft, and the Navy for bombs on ships and Admiralty property, and mines (including those enemy mines that were dropped by air on civilian targets). This left the Army having responsibility for all other enemy bombs (and later recovery of Britain's own defensive land mines).

To start with, the RAF bomb disposal squads were far more experienced than their colleagues in the Army. In fact it was their training school at RAF Manby in Lincolnshire where most of the Royal Engineers received their initial training in bomb disposal, such as it was. The first UXBs to be dealt with, in the Shetlands, had been recovered by an RAF non-commissioned officer the previous year. They were very well aware that bombs would on occasion fail to explode; tests of British ordnance had proved that well. There was also the problem of dealing with UXBs that had been jettisoned from Allied aircraft or were left in them after a crash landing. Indeed, it was dealing with homegrown ordnance that dominated the work of RAF bomb disposal squads. Overall, the contribution of the RAF bomb disposal teams to the success of the Allies in the Battle of Britain cannot be overestimated.

However, the majority of unexploded bombs fell on civilian targets and the responsibility for their disposal fell to the Army. Traditionally, the job of dealing with ordnance, whether unexploded or not, had always fallen to the Royal Army Ordnance Corps. It was decided that the Corps of Royal Engineers were more suited. The skills required for the job had been developed by the RE in the course of their singular history – a history unrivalled by any other branch of the armed forces. They can directly trace their roots back 900 years to the military engineers who arrived in England with the last enemy invasion of the country, by William the Conqueror in 1066. Since then, their service to Crown and country has been unbroken. The motto of the Corps is 'Ubique' – 'Everywhere' – and was awarded by King William IV in 1832 to signify that the Corps had taken part in every battle ever fought by the British Army.

The type of work for which the Engineers are famed was first 'illustrated' in the Bayeux Tapestry, where William's chief engineer can be seen building a prefabricated fort that had been brought with the invading army from Normandy. That building has long been lost, but the White Tower within the Tower of London and Gundulph's Tower at Rochester Cathedral are both early examples of buildings constructed by the precursor to the present-day Corps.

Early methods of warfare became more sophisticated; the arrival of the cannon brought with it a requirement for a body to control the king's cannon, arsenals and fortifications. The first master of this body – the Board of Ordnance – was Nicholas Merbury, who had been chief engineer to Henry V at Agincourt. Engineer officers learnt most of their skills on the Continent, as the Military Academy was not established until 1741. These skills included building trenches, also known as saps – hence the enduring nickname, 'sappers'. The board gained regimental status and was styled the Regiment of Artillery and the Corps of Engineers until the two were separated in the early eighteenth century. It took another sixty years until in 1787 the title Royal was added. At this time the workforce were civilian tradesmen who were recruited according to the requirements of the campaign. Officers, who earned their commissions on merit (unlike those in other regiments who purchased theirs), formed the Corps itself.

It was not until 1772 that the Ordnance board were persuaded that a permanent body of skilled tradesmen, who were subject to military discipline and training, was necessary. Eventually these soldiers were renamed as the Royal Sappers and Miners and they continued to work closely with the Royal Corps of Engineers until 1856, when they were fully incorporated into what is the present Corps of Royal Engineers. Technically, all those who serve in the Royal Engineers, whether officers or soldiers, are known as sappers. However, soldiers who in other regiments would have the rank of private are known as sappers in the Royal Engineers. Officers are referred to by their rank with the initials RE after their name, signifying that they are sapper officers.

In times of war – and increasingly in peacetime – the Royal Engineers support the Army in work that in normal circumstances would be done by civilians. This includes building accommodation, roads, bridges, railways and even harbours. Their training in architecture and design has led to some unexpected commissions including the Royal Albert Hall and Pentonville Prison. But the biggest challenge for the Corps was the work they were to undertake during the Second

World War. They were to provide crucial support in every theatre of war and often entered enemy territory far in advance of other troops. Prior to the invasion of Normandy in 1944, the Royal Engineers used their skills to reconnoitre enemy beaches, providing data for the maps that were essential to a successful Allied landing. During the invasion itself, they were responsible for one of the greatest military engineering feats ever undertaken: the construction of the Mulberry Harbour, which was built in England and towed to Normandy to provide a floating 'port' to supply, reinforce and evacuate the Allied armies.

With their long history of building and demolition, and training in the uses of ordnance, it was entirely logical that the responsibility for bomb disposal would fall to the Royal Engineers. The Formation Order of May 1940 created the first twenty-five sections, each of which comprised an officer, sergeant and fourteen other ranks or sappers. Reality began to bite in June and it became obvious that the problem of UXBs might be far larger than originally expected. A further 109 sections were authorized, the majority of which were 'posted in' with the officers being seconded straight from the Officer Cadet Training Unit. By the end of July the number of sections had increased to 220, formed into companies of ten sections. Each company had its own headquarters and all came under the umbrella of the Inspectorate of Fortifications and Directorate of Bomb Disposal which quickly came to be known as IF&DBD or 'Ifs and Buts'. At its head was the sapper officer Major General G. B. O. Taylor.

As 1940 progressed, the raids were becoming heavier and more frequent. Attacks on London, in what eventually came to be known as the Blitz, started on 29 August 1940.

The Battle of Britain had been raging in the skies over the south-east and London since 8 August. A few days after this, the Luftwaffe was dropping bombs on the airfields from which the Royal Air Force were taking off for their daily sorties. It became clear that there would be some serious disposal challenges ahead – unexploded bombs on an airfield meant that not only were there the obvious destructive consequences, but also that the airfield and all those who worked there were effectively paralyzed.

Bomb disposal in the early days was hampered by a position of almost total ignorance of procedure – starting with how to find a suspected UXB in the first place. Often it was difficult to determine if a hole that had been reported had been caused by a bomb that had exploded, or by one that had not. If a UXB was suspected, the next decision was where to dig the shaft to reach it – not as clear-cut as it may seem, for bombs rarely fell perpendicularly. As a bomb was released from an aircraft, its design and momentum meant that it continued to travel forward, hitting the ground at an angle. The impact would slow the speed of the bomb considerably but, depending on the type of soil, it would continue to travel under the ground for some distance, and possibly to a considerable depth. In the early stages of bomb disposal, a long metal pole would be used to probe down into the hole, following the angle at which the ground had been disturbed. Sometimes, with luck, this would locate the bomb, and the best place for digging the hole could be gauged.

Lack of knowledge was exacerbated by a chronic scarcity of the equipment required to do the job. Just getting to the bombsite often proved difficult – bomb disposal sections were reduced to hitching lifts in civilian cars. Their 'technical equipment' amounted to a pick-axe and shovel for the rank and file, while for the officers, whose job it was to make the bomb safe, a hammer and chisel would have to do.

This shambolic state of affairs was experienced by Stuart Archer when, as an Acting Lieutenant, he arrived in Cardiff in May 1940. He and his section were billeted with the Welsh Regiment and, perhaps somewhat fortunately, they had to walk to the unexploded bombs that were reported to them.

In the middle of the night, about four o'clock, somebody came up to me in my bed and shook me by the shoulder and said, 'You're bomb disposal, aren't you?' I said, 'Yes.' 'Well, there's a bomb on the docks we'd like you to go down and have a look at.' I got up and they drove me down there to see this hole in the ground. I had not heard about the possibility of bombs actually being other than lying in front of me on a table to be dissected. There was something like a two-foot diameter hole, five or six feet deep. So I said yes, that, I suppose, is a bomb. So they took me back to the Welsh Regiment headquarters, the sergeant and men got up out of bed and started to march down towards this bomb site with their pick-axe and shovels over their shoulders, and on the way the bomb went off. That was really quite a surprise to everybody.

His own thoughts as to the lucky escape he had just experienced were somewhat sanguine: 'The only thing that I can remember as far as my own reactions are concerned, is that later that day I phoned my wife and said, "I am going to get a place for you to come down here and live because it doesn't look like I'm going to last very long!"'

In the early summer of 1940, before the start of the blitz on London, the Royal Engineers had already embarked on a very steep learning curve. Bombing continued to be light into June, with only twenty UXBs needing their attention. July saw an increase to 1,000, and during August a further 300 were dealt with. The Royal Engineers were working as fast as they could, but by the end of August there were over 2,000 bombs awaiting their attention, a number that was to increase to a staggering 3,759 by the end of September 1940.

Digging for a bomb was to bring its own challenges. Holes could not be dug straight down without the risk of the sides collapsing, and digging in most soil types required the use of wooden shoring. It was also important that the type and size of the bomb be ascertained. This mattered little from a safety point of view: given the close proximity in which the men worked, an explosion would be devastating for them whatever the size of bomb. The size did, however, give some pointers to the type of fuze that it might contain. As we will see later, this was to become the crucial issue for bomb disposal.

Sometimes the entry hole would be enough to determine the size of the bomb. During the excavations, finding the bomb's tail fins would confirm this. The tail fins were attached to the rear of the bomb and enabled it to hold a steady trajectory on leaving the aircraft. Screws or small rivets attached them to the bomb and, as it moved through the ground, they would detach. The size of the tail fins related directly to the size of the bomb; once this was established, preparations would be made for the next stage in making it safe.

German high explosive aerial bombs came in many forms. The smallest and most common was the 50-kilogram (110-pound) bomb. There were many other sizes to be dealt with and many were to be dubbed with nicknames appropriate to the time. They included the 100-kilogram (220-pound), 250-kilogram (550-pound), 500-kilogram (1,100-pound), 1,000-kilogram (2,200-pound) known as 'Hermann', 1,400-kilogram (3,080-pound) or 'Fritz', ending with the enormous and aptly named 'Satan', which weighed in at 1,800 kilograms (3,960 pounds). The bombs were of two different types: the SC and the SD. The SC bomb had a thin metal casing and was used for general bombing over urban and civilian areas. The SD type, with a much thicker case, was designed for use as an armour-piercing bomb – ideal for penetrating shipping or buildings where maximum damage was required.

The explosive element of an SC bomb amounted to half its total weight, while in an SD bomb it was about one-third. The filling used differed little from that used in British bombs. It was put into the bomb via a base plate that screwed into place and came in three types: TNT, amatol or aluminized powder. All these explosives are very stable and require considerable force to detonate them. It was the German electrical fuze in its many guises which was to provide this power, and it was one which was to form the basis for the war between the British bomb disposal officer and the German fuze designer.

The extensive developments in fuze technology that the Germans had undertaken in the decade and a half before the war had resulted in a large number of different types of fuzes. Each one was designed in Germany for a specific purpose, and the challenge for the British was to find the method of making it safe. While many of the fuzes had been developed far in advance of the Second World War, recently discovered documentary evidence has provided proof that intelligence filtering back to Germany from Britain directly affected the technology. Not only were variations made to existing fuzes, but also completely new ones were developed. This contrasted with Hitler's edict early in the war which forbade any investment in developments that would take longer than a year to complete, so confident was he of an early Allied surrender.

Indeed, after the end of the war, General Ernst Marquard, who had been in charge of the Luftwaffe's bombing strategy, wrote a report for the American government which showed the importance attached to staying one step ahead of the game: 'The English government soon realized the threat of our unexploded bombs, and renowned scientists developed methods to defuze them. On our side, every attempt was made to foil these measures, and so the guerrilla war with bombs continued.'

Ironically, the information regarding the basic operation of German fuzes was available for public view in London, had anybody thought to look for it. An application under the title *Electric Time and Impact Fuzes for projectiles and the like* had been lodged with the patents office in thirty-five different territories, including the United Kingdom, by a German company called Rheinmetall. It was a statistic of which the inventor of the electric fuze, Herbert Erich Ruehlemann, was extremely proud.

What was it about the electric fuze that made it so effective a means of detonating a bomb? It was essentially no more effective than the mechanical version used by the Royal Air Force. In fact, although the British fuze was more primitive, its unpredictable performance often made it more effective – in causing chaos rather than destruction, that is. The German fuzes, by contrast, were more precise in their manufacture, and so more effective; but once they had been analysed and a means of defuzing discovered, they were more consistent to deal with. The fuze itself was slotted into a pocket in the side of the bomb. At its head, where the fuze number was imprinted, there were two spring-loaded plungers. The bombs were loaded on to racks inside the aircraft and were attached to the fuze head by two sockets. As the bomb fell from the aircraft, the battery in the bomb bay charged the capacitor in the fuze. This could happen only when the socket was jerked free as the bomb fell; thus a charged fuze – and thereby a primed bomb – would never remain in the aircraft.

As the bomb fell through the air, the charge passed through a resistor into a firing capacitor. The bomb was now armed. The aircraft was well out of danger of being caught in any explosion by the time this transfer of energy had taken place. Within the firing capacitor there was an impact switch that closed when the bomb hit the ground. With the closing of this switch, the circuit was complete: a spark would pass through an explosive booster pellet and ignite a small amount of explosive in the gaine (a small 'cup' screwed into the bottom of the fuze) which would in turn generate enough energy to explode the bomb. In order for this type of fuze to work effectively, there must be enough time between the bomb leaving the aircraft and hitting the ground for the sequence to be completed. Therefore, if a bomb was dropped from too low an altitude it would not be fully charged. However, it still had to be considered dangerous. The resistor would continue to allow energy to pass through into the firing capacitor, so any sudden jolt could cause the impact switch to close. This meant that while the bomb itself could be relatively inert, it had to be treated with respect.

The development of the electric fuze had been a long process. Ruehlemann's quest for the perfect means of detonating a bomb had started at the request of the German government in the 1920s to find a more efficient artillery shell. Money was no object and with the backing of Rheinmetall, one of the most powerful manufacturing companies in Germany, employing over 100,000 people. His research department became key to the Nazi war effort and was based at Rheinmetall's plant in Sömmerda. Ruehlemann himself was so highly regarded that not only was he given the Iron Cross but he was personally given 50,000 marks by Herman Goering in recognition of his work.

Artillery shells were fired into the air and designed to explode in or near their target to cause maximum damage. The electrical means of detonation meant that a tiny delay could be introduced – somewhere in the region of 0.8 seconds after impact – which would allow the shell to explode at a safe distance from the point of firing. It was decided in 1932 to incorporate this technology into bombs that were designed to be dropped from aircraft. Extensive testing of the new fuze technology took place in Russia during July of that year. Germany was still forbidden to develop any weapons under the Treaty of Versailles, but an agreement between the German and Russian governments meant that in return for allowing the testing to take place within the Russians' borders, Germany would provide them with duplicates of all the materials used in the tests. The testing was being carried out at the request of the German Navy but interest in the technology was immense and the key decision maker for the Luftwaffe, General Ernst Marquard, was also in attendance. It was he who was to become Ruehlemann's biggest customer.

The whole testing operation was shrouded in the most intense secrecy. Getting all relevant personnel and equipment to the proofing ground, near the small town of Lipezk, 800 kilometres (nearly 500 miles) south of Moscow, was a logistical triumph. This involved disguised aircraft, and personnel leaving from different railway stations over the course of a week as it was vital that suspicions weren't aroused in Germany where Allied agents were already reporting 'unusual' activities back to the British government.

At this time, dropping bombs from aircraft was a new type of weapon. Little was known about their accuracy, ballistic properties or the speed at which they might travel. Most of the tests were carried out using 50-kilogram bombs. The focus of the testing was to find out the optimum length of delay necessary between a bomb hitting the ground and exploding. Various timings were tried. The bomb had to penetrate the ground far enough to cause maximum damage but not so far that the ground would insulate the explosion. After weeks of testing, dropping bombs from aircraft, a delay of 0.005 seconds was determined to be the optimum. Ruehlemann was delighted with the test results. It was the breakthrough he had been waiting for. There had not been one failure during all the tests. The Navy made an immediate decision to adopt the new fuze, and the Luftwaffe under the direction of General Marquard was soon to follow.

Marquard and Ruehlemann's professional relationship developed into friendship and the two travelled extensively to promote the new technology in the 1930s. Sales were made, unsurprisingly, to the Italians and the Japanese, who both purchased licences under which they were to develop their own fuzes. Perhaps more surprising is that Ruehlemann visited both Britain and the United States in the three years immediately preceding the war. His visit to Britain included a trip to an air show on the outskirts of London. The main event was a restricted display open only to invited guests where the full power of newly developed aircraft was on display. Representatives of Rheinmettal, expressly forbidden by the terms of the Treaty of Versailles from manufacturing weapons, were definitely not invited. Nevertheless, Ruehlemann, using half a ticket obtained from a friendly Dutch industrialist and tucked into the top of his jacket pocket, gained entry, passing the guards with confidence to see what the rest of the world's technology had to offer. He left impressed and aware that the aircraft industry worldwide was preparing itself for war.

Ruehlemann's trip to the United States was at the instigation of Ernst von Siemens, whose company worked closely with Ruehlemann in his development of the electric fuze, providing vital components and support. Ruehlemann hoped to achieve two objectives on this trip: the sale of the electric fuze to the United States military, and knowledge about developments in resistors and condensers, of which he believed the USA to be at the vanguard. His first objective involved demonstrating the electric bomb fuze at the War Department in Washington DC as well as at the Army's foremost proofing ground at Aberdeen, Maryland. All the demonstrations were observed by high-ranking officers of the Army, Navy and Air Force including General Tschapper, the Chief of the War Department at the time. Ruehlemann was also given guided tours of factories belonging to General Electric, Westinghouse, the Ford Motor Company and Bell Laboratories. While he was most impressed with their organization, he was disappointed with the quality of their condensers and resistors – those available in Germany were far superior. Later, however, in the factory at Sömmerda in eastern Germany, he was quick to introduce the production line systems and factory lay-outs he had seen.

The factory at Sömmerda was funded by the Nazi party and, with the co-operation of such well-known names as electrical giant Siemens and Rosenthal, the china company that supplied the high-grade porcelain needed for the condensers, it went on to produce vast numbers of fuzes. The factories were staffed by 'guest workers' from Poland, France and Czechoslovakia who lived on site and were seemingly well looked after. Millions of fuzes were manufactured and under his contract Ruehlemann was entitled to a royalty – which in fact he never received. Even in the latter part of his life it still rankled that he was several million marks out of pocket.

The electrical fuze was used throughout the war and was regarded as one of the Nazi war machine's finest inventions. There was only one safety alarm raised, when it was reported that an aircraft had exploded in mid air after its bombs had been released. This led to a massive recall of tens of thousands of fuzes to find the fault. There was even a suggestion of sabotage. This was very unlikely, however, as the system of checking and numbering meant that each fuze could be traced back to a specific day, time and person. In the end it was discovered that the pilot had himself been rather overzealous in the use of his machine-guns and, as the bombs had fallen away, he had inadvertently hit one of them exactly on its fuse.

Ruehlemann was to visit Britain once more, after the war when he was interrogated about his work in Germany. The years that followed the Allied victory in Europe saw the beginnings of a new world order.

America, despite being a wartime ally, was eager to beat Russia in the post-war distribution of Nazi scientists. Their experimental work in the fields of rocketry, electronics and biology, though morally dubious, was a very valuable commodity. A covert operation, codenamed 'Paperclip', was instituted and scientists whose work had been carried out in the name of the Nazi party had their records sanitized. Many of the German elite, their Nazi history expunged, became 'refugees', a status that allowed them to work in the United States free from enquiries about their true history.

Ruehlemann was part of this influx of European know-how and returned to the Aberdeen Proofing Ground in Maryland, where he had once demonstrated the electric fuze, to work in bomb development from 1948 until 1955. However, unlike his more high-profile colleagues such as the rocket scientist Werner von Braun, who was key to America being the first to land men on the moon, Ruehlemann's security clearance was never high enough to allow him further promotion within the military. He ended his career working for a firm of engineers in Pennsylvania, in the employ of a Belgian Jew.

2

The challenge begins

So these unexploded bombs, in some ways, created a more lasting problem for society than the bomb that had come down and gone off. This was a very clever move on the part of the Germans: it altered the character and increased the impact of their raids.

MAJOR JOHN HUDSON

ONCE THE DECISION HAD BEEN MADE to establish a cohesive force for bomb disposal operations, the Royal Engineers under the direction of the Inspectorate of Fortifications and Directorate of Bomb Disposal were quick to respond. Major General Taylor was in his position as the Director of IF&DBD on 29 August 1940 – also the day that the Blitz started over London. His task was to oversee the formation of an adequate infrastructure: easier said than done. The force of the bombardment was a shock to all. The most pessimistic could not have foretold the mass devastation that the Luftwaffe were to bring. Even Winston Churchill, whose prescience in all matters of war was to become legendary, was taken by surprise. Thankfully, he quickly realized that the problem of bomb disposal could be considerable, and moved the issue to the top of his personal and political agenda. In a memo to the Minister of Supply dated 21 September 1940 and copied to the key members of the War Cabinet, he said:

The rapid disposal of unexploded bombs is of the highest importance. Any failure to grapple with this problem may have serious results on the production of aircraft, and other vital war material. The work of the Bomb Disposal Squads must be facilitated by the provision of every kind of up-to-date equipment.

Churchill continued to take a keen interest in developments in bomb disposal, requiring almost daily reports on the numbers of bombs dealt with and the casualties reported. He even passed on information regarding an augur he had seen in the United States. He thought this machine – like a giant corkscrew – might be useful in speeding up excavations for bombs, and personally sanctioned the ordering of several.

In a personal memo to the Secretary of State for War, Churchill wrote regarding one bombing raid:

War Office have accepted from the War Cabinet the responsibility of dealing with delayed action bombs. This may become a feature of the enemy attack. A number were thrown last night into the City causing obstruction. They may even try them on Whitehall! It seems to me that an energetic effort should be made to provide sufficient squads to deal with this form of attack in the large centres. The squads must be highly mobile so as not to waste men and material. They must move in motor lorries quickly from one point to another.

The delayed action bombs to which Churchill was referring had already been causing problems in other parts of the country, most notably in Wales. The Germans used them sparingly, as the fuze needed was not only more complicated but was also larger and could be fitted only into bombs larger than 50 kilograms. However, despite accounting for only a small percentage of the number of bombs dropped, its arrival fundamentally changed the way each and every bombsite had to be treated. Until this time, a UXB with an impact fuze (numbered 15) could be neutralized quickly by carefully depressing the two spring-loaded plungers on the fuze head and removing the fuze. The bomb would then be taken to a safe place where the explosive filling was either burnt out or exploded. TNT, which was the most common filling, could be set alight without any risk of explosion.

Of course, there was still an element of risk: a residual charge in the fuze could leak through, thereby exploding the bomb. But the delayed action fuze, which included a clockwork mechanism and was numbered 17, fulfilled a very different function. When dropped on urban and industrial targets, it was designed to cause maximum disruption. The Luftwaffe's General Marquard was quick to realize how effective a delayed action bomb could be. In a report he wrote for the American government after the War, he noted: 'We realized that an electric clockwork fuze which could be set up to ignite up to seventy-two hours after falling would cause disruption to the enemy's armaments industry, to transport and to the general public, and would tie up considerable bomb disposal resources.'

The recovery and examination of the first number 17 fuze in the middle of August 1940 was to open a new chapter for bomb disposal. The Research Department at the Woolwich Arsenal were quick to find out how it worked, but still desperately needed more fuzes on which to experiment. Once the clockwork element was discovered, the experiments that were to lead to the magnetic clock-stopper were soon under way. Testing this new technique was vital to its success.

Each fuze could be set with a delay of between one and seventy-two hours. If every UXB had to be regarded as possibly containing a number 17 fuze that could detonate at any time up to three days after it was dropped, then all but the most vital of sites would be left alone until the danger period had passed: roads would be closed, railway lines suspended, factories shut down and people kept away from their homes. Finding more complete fuzes to study became the highest priority.

Bombs had already been categorized according to their priority:

A1 Immediate disposal essential. Detonation of the bomb in situ cannot be accepted on any terms.
A2 Immediate disposal essential. Bomb may, if the situation demands it, be detonated in situ.
B   Rapid disposal urgent, but less urgent than A.
C   Not necessarily calling for immediate action.
D   May be dealt with as convenient.

Bombs in factories, near major transport arteries or communications installations such as telephone exchanges generally fell into the top two categories. Aerodromes holding aircraft essential to the Battle of Britain clearly fell into the A1 category, and it was in such a place, in Wales, that Lieutenant Stuart Archer found himself ordered to recover a bomb 'at all costs'. As we saw in the last chapter, his early days in bomb disposal had already thrown up some unexpected events, but things were about to get even more demanding.

Archer had been posted to Swansea in the early summer of 1940 and he and his section were very busy over the first couple of months. He remembers that in the early days nearly every bomb and fuze that was found was new to the officer finding it. His section, like all the others, had been issued with a two-pin discharger, called a Crabtree discharger, to neutralize the bombs. It wasn't long before he was made aware that using it could have fatal results. The 'luck' that Archer characterizes most of his time in bomb disposal was very much in evidence here.

Two or three months later the Germans brought out a fuze numbered 25. If you used a two-pin discharger on that, the thing would blow up. As with all the things I was doing, pure luck came into it. I got out a 25 fuze, sent it up to the War Office and within two days a teleprinter came round saying, 'Don't put a Crabtree on a 25 fuze.'

Archer was well aware how important it was at this time that as many complete fuzes as possible were recovered for research purposes. It was obvious to most sappers, who were trained in demolition, how easy it would be to incorporate some kind of booby-trap into a fuze. For this reason a string was usually tied to the fuze head and it was extracted from a distance. Eventually a more sophisticated system of pulley and wheels was introduced, called a Merrylees fuze extractor, but it was still a question of finding the booby-trap before it found them. The fuze that fitted the bill arrived bearing the number 50: an anti-disturbance fuze that would detonate the bomb at the slightest movement and was seemingly irremovable. Using the Merrylees was not always practical. Archer had unwittingly come across a number 50 and attached a cord:

It had a different number but that didn't mean anything to me. I tried with the cord to pull the fuze out and it wouldn't come. It was jammed. But, nevertheless, because this was one of the fuzes that the War Office asked us to produce, what I managed to do was to force it out and I used, believe it or not, two pick heads to sort of move it half an inch. Then I was able to pull it out with a spanner.

The fuze had malfunctioned and only by yet another incredible stroke of luck was he able to provide the scientists back at the Ministry of Supply and the research establishment at Woolwich with their precious fuze. Realizing what the 50 fuze now did changed the way in which bombs were located. The original method, using the long probe to push down through the ground and make contact with the bomb case, was no longer an option. The slightest tapping could detonate the bomb. Life was getting more and more difficult for all concerned. But it was still the 17 that was causing the most problems, as Stuart Archer had already found out.

The raids had been getting heavier and concentrating on South Wales for some time. The area provided huge amounts of coal to the rest of Britain, and its major ports were home to several oil refineries. There has even been speculation that Hitler planned to base his post-invasion government there. St Athan's aerodrome was on Archer's 'patch' in July 1940 and was home to a large number of aircraft that were about to be used in the Battle of Britain. The aerodrome was a category A1 location and, as such, the two UXBs that were there had to be dealt with 'at all costs'. Both contained 17 fuzes and as one had not yet been recovered intact, there was still no means of telling whether they were ticking or not.

They were 17 fuzes and we obviously couldn't leave them to go off. It was also dangerous to attempt to extract the fuzes while they were there adjoining this building, because that was also likely to set the bomb off. So, we took the last and foolish way of going about it. The only way was to actually dig up the bomb, put it on the back of our lorry, drive it away and blow it up somewhere else. This is what we did with each of the bombs.

Archer is self-effacing regarding the courage required to do this: 'One only had one person driving the lorry and as I was the one taking the decisions, I drove the lorry. I was not being brave really. You didn't really want the men to think that you were sending somebody away with a live bomb. A lot of my friends have done this. There's nothing very special about it.'

The bombs were blown up a couple of miles away in a farmer's field. Number 17 fuzes were still required for research, and once again Stuart Archer was to find himself at the centre of events when he managed to recover yet another variation on the number 17. This time the Germans had added a device that seemed to make removing the fuze virtually impossible.

The bombing had almost reached the height of its destructive powers, with cities the length and breadth of the country being pounded nightly by vast waves of German bombers. Llandarcy Oil Refinery near Swansea was nearly forty miles from where Archer and his section were based in Cardiff. They received notification of unexploded bombs at eight o'clock one morning and arrived at the site two hours later. Finding their way had not been difficult: the fires could be seen from 20 miles away and the vast plumes of smoke were a portent of what was to come.

When we arrived we were told that there were four unexploded bombs in the oil refinery in what was known as the tank farm. These were large gasometer-like steel tanks holding fuel. There were four bombs laid in a straight line which had been dropped in what was called a 'stick'. I looked at all four and decided we could only tackle one anyway with my little group. The one to tackle was right by the side of one of the oil tanks. It had in fact broken through the concrete base of the tank itself. Only fifty or so yards away was an oil tank which was on fire, so the heat was enormous and the excitement terrific.

The smoke was so thick that in almost obscured the sun. The men started to dig.

It was hot and because it was really a rather emotional thing just being there, I had the men working only quarter-hour shifts. I stayed there on the site of the bomb to give them confidence. After two hours, at about midday, the nearest of the other bombs exploded. It didn't do any damage but it did make us realize that what we had got was probably something similar.

They continued digging and, on uncovering the bomb, saw the fuze had been damaged, causing the fuze head to shear off. There was nothing to see and no way of telling what kind of fuze they were dealing with. It was also impossible to remove the fuze. Archer decided to tackle the problem in a different way. At the blunt end of each bomb was a base plate through which the bomb was filled with explosive. If it could be removed, it was possible to scrape out the explosive. However, removing the base plate involved considerable movement which could, of course, detonate the bomb.

As one couldn't tell what it was, I thought I would tackle it by another means, which was most unorthodox but a possibility. I unscrewed the steel base plate and found that this exposed the explosive. It so happened that the explosive was powdered. So with a trowel, digging away, I got the explosive out and that exposed the fuze pocket which ran across the diameter of the bomb. The left-hand side of the fuze pocket has been damaged and had almost torn away. On the other side the fuze pocket was just attached to the bomb case by a little spot weld and that wasn't a very strong one. So, by moving and getting my arm down inside the bomb, I was able to hold the fuze pocket and with brute force and bloody ignorance bang it back and forth until I got the whole thing free.

All the while the fire had continued to rage and the other bombs had exploded. At last, the researchers would have another 17 fuze to work on. Archer examined the fuze and was very surprised to find even more than he had expected.

I took the fuze pocket away and tried to pull the fuze out with my fingers but there were only little bits of wire sticking up. So I got some pliers and I pulled and there on the back end of it was the 17 clock – ticking! Then I looked down the tube and there was another strange object. I put my pliers down and tried to take hold but couldn't, so I tried to shake the thing out. Eventually, with tapping the fuze pocket on a rail nearby, I managed to get it and as it was coming out there was a 'crack'.

Not only had he recovered a ticking 17 fuze, he had also unwittingly uncovered the device that so far had prevented it being removed: the Zus40 anti-withdrawal. The crack he had heard was the

Zus40 firing, which should have caused the fuze to fire when he attempted to pull the 17 out. Luckily the gaine was far enough away not to matter on this occasion. It would seem that some water had found its way into the damaged fuze pocket and created enough moisture to dampen the explosive charge in the device.

Archer sums up his achievement most succinctly: 'I had our lovely prize: a 17 fuze and the first Zus40 to come out in one piece. Lots of people had pulled them out before but they had been blown up, whereas I hadn't. This was luck, luck, luck.'

For his incredible luck and corresponding courage, Archer was to receive a new award instituted in September the following year, which recognized exceptional courage on the home front: the George Cross, equivalent to the Victoria Cross for valour in the field. Churchill himself had noted the need for acknowledging the nature of the work: 'The service which is highly dangerous must be considered particularly honourable, and rewards should follow its successful discharge.' In the citation that accompanied Archer's award, General Taylor, the director of the Inspectorate of Fortifications and Directorate of Bomb Disposal, said: 'The fact that Lieutenant Archer has enjoyed such remarkable immunity from death in no way detracts from his record of deliberate and sustained courage coupled with devotion to duty of the highest order.'

The earlier recovery of the 17 fuze had resulted in the beginning of the development of the magnetic clock-stopper. A very cumbersome but effective means of making the bomb temporarily safe, it was invented by a Mr Samson, who worked for the General Electric Company. Major John Hudson remembers the thinking behind this piece of equipment.

The only way that anybody could think of preventing this fuze from going off was to stop the clock. It's very difficult to stop the clock, which is of course inside a large metal casing. It was found that it was quite possible to stop the clock by applying a magnet, which would draw the steel spindles in the clock up against the bearings and create enough friction for the spring not to be able to turn the cogs. The first attempt was an appalling piece of apparatus. It was an incredibly clumsy way of stopping a clock, but was one of the breakthroughs for bomb disposal.

Although in short supply, they were a boon to the bomb disposal sections at the time. However, there were complications. Bombs with two fuze pockets began to appear.

In general, the combination of fuzes that were fitted was a 17 and a 50, the first being the time delay and the second the anti-handling fuze that required a movement of less than a millimetre to activate the trembler switch. The process of attaching the unwieldy clock-stopper was more than enough to cause the 50 fuze to detonate. Yet again, the researchers under the direction of the Unexploded Bomb Committee came up with a solution. It was here that the BD discharger with its mixture of alcohol, benzine and salt came into play. Once the solution was forced into the fuze and it was left for the required thirty minutes, the fuze would become inert and the clock-stopper could be attached. This method was developed by Major C. A. J. Martin, who worked with Flying Officer John Rowlands (later to become Air Marshal Sir John Rowlands). Sir John, who also attended meetings of the Unexploded Bomb Committee, remembers the method his colleague developed well.

Now once we had immunized that fuze – and bear in mind there was only one person allowed to work at the bomb at a time – then from a distance we used to give a little tug to the bomb to make sure the 50 had actually been neutralized. When that was done we could turn our attention to the 17. It was very simple to begin with: we merely unscrewed the locking plate and took the fuze out – the bomb was safe.

The Zus40 complicated matters.

*Once again we had to concentrate on the long delay fuze. What
we did with this was to prepare a very quick setting material. A
vacuum pump was attached to the fuze head and clamped on
to the bomb with rubber seals. When all the air was forced out
a toggle was pulled and this very quick setting plastic was fed
into the fuze pocket. Once it had set then you could pull the
fuzes out. All this was done by remote control in case the bomb
went off.*

All these inventions had been developed very quickly by scientists
both military and civilian. The Unexploded Bomb Committee had
been formed to co-ordinate these developments and was the fiefdom
of its chairman Dr H. J. Gough, the Director General of Scientific
Research and Development, a directorate within the Ministry of
Supply. The financial and developmental responsibilities relating to
bomb disposal had been delegated to the Ministry of Supply since 1
April 1940. Control prior to this time had been with the Ministry of
Home Security and very little developmental work had been carried
out. At the time, it seemed not to be needed. Until now, the specialist
tools had been limited to the two-pin discharger (the Crabtree), and
an adjustable key for removing the locking ring from the top of the
fuze pocket.

The 17 fuze had caused a heightened sense of alarm. More than
ever, the all-clear siren was not a reliable signal – bombs could be
heard exploding for up to three days after a raid. The Unexploded
Bomb Committee decided to create a Research and Development Sub-
committee, which did not come into being until October 1940.
Among the first devices to be invented was the steam sterilizer which
was designed to cut a hole in the top of the bomb casing and then
emulsify the explosive before forcing it out of the bomb case under
pressure. The machine did all this work, while personnel remained at
a safe distance. Dr Gough, Dr A. D. Merriman (who had defuzed the
first two UXBs recovered at Sullom Voe in November 1939), and two
other colleagues from the Royal Engineers and the Unexploded Bomb

Committee first used this equipment on a bomb in London's Regent Street in September 1940. The bomb they were dealing with had two fuze pockets, both of which contained type 17 fuzes. One was ticking. It took several hours to get the machinery working correctly and all the time the fuze was ticking its way towards explosion. Gough and his colleagues were watching from a bunker made of sandbags when after four hours of work the bomb blew up – but much had been learned: the operation was viewed as a definite success.

As pointed out earlier, finding bombs was also a big problem. Apart from the difficulty of establishing the bomb's actual location after it had travelled through the earth, probing was difficult and dangerous due to the sensitivity of the 50 anti-handling fuze, and the advent of the type 17 fuze often meant that the bomb had to be found more quickly. Without the benefit of metal-detector technology, the Unexploded Bomb Committee were willing to listen to anyone who had good news regarding bomb locating. One of the more eccentric attempts was by a man called Maby, who in his Gloucestershire home had been investigating the use of dowsing as a means of locating bombs. Such was his enthusiasm that in February 1942 Professor E. N. da C. Andrade was dispatched to see if his claims amounted to anything. The professor's report sadly came to the conclusion that 'the scientific basis of Mr Maby's claims is ridiculous' and that he was 'at the most favourable a self-deceiving enthusiast, but a less favourable point of view could be supported'. However, a handwritten note on one copy of the report was more appreciative, thanking Professor Andrade for sending it as 'I haven't had such a good laugh in ages.'

Back in 1940 the issue of the 17 fuze was still causing problems. The clock-stopper and BD discharger were all very well once you had located the bomb. What would happen if you could not wait the three days required and had to continue digging to expose the fuze?

Lieutenant Eric Wakeling, who as described in the last chapter started his Royal Engineers career in chemical warfare, was only twenty years old when he was posted to bomb disposal. He was well aware of the realities of the war that was being fought and that it depended on machinery being built and ready on time: 'I think the German thinking at the time was not to get at us but to hold up the war effort. I mean you could always replace people; you can't always replace equipment. We were expendable and I think we realized that too.'

He found himself in a dilemma when he attended a category A1 bombsite in a factory making tanks. The equipment had all been imported from the United States and was irreplaceable. The orders were to remove the bomb 'at all costs' without it exploding. The report had come through at three o'clock in the morning, and Wakeling told the guard to wake up his section. Five minutes later he was briefing them in the section office, laying out the operation for which he had already made provision. His plans were to use three squads working in shifts. He dispatched the first squad with a compressor, as there was a concrete floor that would have to be cut through before work could start. The second section followed with the timber required to shore up the sides of the shaft that would be dug down to the bomb.

Wakeling arrived at the site to be met by a man from the Ministry of Supply who impressed on the young officer how important it was that the machinery be preserved. Wakeling's next task was finding the bomb.

All this concrete, all these machines, hardly room to put a hole, dig a shaft... When you find the hole of entry for a bomb it is at an angle. Most people think bombs come straight down. They don't. They never hit the vertical. They're always at an angle and you have to find the angle using a probe, a metal rod that you stick down this hole and you get the angle of entry. Then you say, we'll dig a shaft there.

Wakeling and his section were in luck. The hole could be dug between some machinery: 'We got cracking with the pneumatic drills and I thought, my God, if there's a 50 fuze down there is it going to go off with all this vibration? It was a possibility.'

It took many hours for the bomb to be uncovered, during which time very little sleep or food was had by anyone. Wakeling did, however, manage a short break and on his way back into the factory his sergeant met him: 'He had sent the men away and probed down and actually touched the bomb. He put an electromagnetic stethoscope on the probe and had heard it was ticking. He had pulled the probe out, called the men back and told them to get on with the work.'

Wakeling then had to decide whether to tell the men about the bomb's state. He decided that honesty was the least they were owed.

We went back to the shaft and I said to the men, 'You've got a ticking fuze down there so start rabitting.' Normally when you dig a shaft you straighten the sides and you have a more or less level floor all the time. Rabitting meant that you just go for the bomb. We knew where it was because it had been probed. We just had to dig a hole big enough to get down to the bomb.

When the bomb was reached, it had been ticking for over eighteen hours. It had two fuzes: a 17 and a 50. First, Wakeling used the BD discharger which took a further thirty minutes to work before the clock-stopper could be employed. Eventually the BD discharger was emptied of liquid and the clock-stopper could be attached with its satisfying clunk. A few hours' more excavation and the bomb was removed with the clock-stopper still attached. It had been a very long day and Wakeling and his section were glad to head to the pub for a celebratory drink.

Wartime was a time of extremes and, while many rose to the challenge, there were also those who felt weighed down by the pressure. When a bomb fell so close to St Paul's Cathedral that it was feared the dome could be brought down, the man hailed as its saviour had his face in every newspaper in the country. The story of how he came to be there, and what happened to him subsequently, belies the simplicity of the heading 'St Paul's Saved'.

On 12 September 1940 the Blitz was at its destructive peak. All over London firewatchers scanned the roofs for incendiaries, floating bombs designed to set fire to property. In St Paul's, that beloved national icon, every available means was employed to extinguish fire – when water and sand were unavailable, even prayer hassocks were used to kill the flames. It wasn't long into the night before a giant hole in Dean's Yard signalled that a deadly UXB was lurking below. The call went out and 105 BD section of 5 Company Royal Engineers arrived at the scene. Lieutenant Robert Davies was in charge and, after surveying the scene, he ordered his men to start digging. Meanwhile, he departed for a breakfast of kippers.

For three days and nights, the men of the section dug a shaft nearly 30 feet (9 metres) deep. It was not long before reinforcements from the Gas Light and Coke Company had to be brought in. Not only was the bomb with its suspected type 17 delayed action fuze shifting in clay atop the very foundations of the cathedral, but it had also fractured a gas main and severed electricity cables as it crashed through the ground. Electric sparks, natural gas and a large amount of TNT made a lethal mix, and the engineers worked around the bomb to make the environment marginally safer. When at last the bomb was exposed Lieutenant Davies returned to the scene. The fuze was ticking.

A type 17 fuze was designed to explode at any time up to seventy-two hours after it was dropped, and that time limit had almost passed. Davies decided that removing the fuze *in situ* was not an option. Instead, he ordered the streets to be cleared from St Paul's to Hackney. The bomb would have to be moved. Sapper George Wylie and his section hauled the 1,000-kilogram bomb from the hole. At any moment it could have exploded, killing them and bringing Wren's magnificent dome crashing down. Their efforts in locating it had already been heroic, and now they managed to load it on to a lorry.

Alone, Davies drove four and a half miles through the deserted streets of east London to Hackney Marshes and its 'bomb cemetery', open ground well away from habitation. The bomb was unloaded and exploded in a controlled detonation, which resulted in a deep crater more than 100 feet wide and 8 feet deep (30 by 2.5 metres).

The propaganda value in such a heroic tale was not ignored by the government and within two days the newspapers were full of the tremendous bravery of Lieutenant Davies and Sapper George Wylie. Both men were awarded the George Cross. But it was the kind of fame with which Davies was not entirely comfortable: 'It seems as though they are trying to make me a national hero,' he wrote to his wife shortly afterwards, 'but don't take any notice of it. I am still the same old dad.'

The pressure of the job seemed to get to one or two of the other men of the section, and in October 1940, just a month after the St Paul's incident, Lieutenant Davies found himself in Clerkenwell Magistrates' Court giving evidence on behalf of Sappers Wilfred Hall and John Gale. Both had been charged with assaulting a policeman and causing damage to the window of a public house. 'We have been working at very high pressure,' stated Davies, 'and with all due respect for the job, it is not the type a lot of people rush after. The men are working in the face of death all the time. I know that my own temper has become somewhat frayed. As soldiers, they are of the best.' The magistrate discharged the men, admitting that there was no doubt they were working under great mental strain.

It would seem that it was not only the humble sappers who were vulnerable to the relentless stress under which they were working. Eighteen months later Robert Davies, now promoted to captain, was to find himself back in court, and this time it was he who was in the dock. The charges were many and various and all of them arose from incidents in 1940. He was accused of looting ladies' underwear from a bombed factory. The newspapers of the time noted pruriently that his batman had been requested to send one package to his wife in Plymouth and another to a woman in Cornwall. There was also the question of money given by the public in thanks for the work of the bomb disposal men. Such gifts were not officially to be accepted, but the correct route for it was into the Royal Engineers Association bank account and not into Captain Davies's pocket. In all there were forty charges, twenty-nine of which related to dishonoured cheques. He was sentenced to eighteen months and cashiered in disgrace from the Army.

Since his very public fall from grace, whispers about the 'true' nature of his part in the saving of St Paul's have flitted around the bomb disposal world. Rumours have abounded that he was not there for any of the excavations or the discovery and extraction of the bomb and that he was drunk and ill-disciplined. It seemed to matter little what was said about a man who had so disgraced himself and the Royal Engineers. He died in 1975 aged seventy-four in the town of Lakemba, New South Wales.

After the original sale of Davies's George Cross in 1970, it passed through several owners before being bought for £90,000 in 1982 by the Charterhouse Bank. Their offices overlook Dean's Yard and St Paul's Cathedral and, in gratitude for the preservation of their magnificent view, they donated the medal to St Paul's collection of artefacts. It may be hard to imagine why anyone would sell a medal, which represented what was, at the time, one of the most famous incidents of the London Blitz. We may never know the real reasons Robert Davies had for parting with such a treasure, but it is true to say that a very public honour hid a very private tragedy.

It was not just the urban areas of the United Kingdom that were affected by unexploded bombs. Luftwaffe bombers would often unload bombs over the countryside, either by mistake or to avoid having to return to base with bombs still on board. To do so could be both hazardous and humiliating for the crew. Bombs that fell in open countryside were not a priority but their disposal was no easier for the bomb disposal officer involved.

John Hannaford was sent to South Wales after his call-up in 1941. His father had been in the Royal Flying Corps in the First World War, and he well remembers queuing at the recruiting centre in Preston with his mind made up that he would join the RAF and train to be a pilot.

I heard one young fellow ahead of me say, 'What do you think you'll go in for?' Well, I was a bit of an aeroplane buff and I told him I'd like to go in the RAF as a pilot. A voice behind me said, 'You know they're looking for rear gunners? Do you know the average life of a rear gunner just now?' He said, 'Three weeks!' By this time I was nearly at the officer's table. He looked up and he said, 'I see you're a trainee architect. What do you think you would like to go in for?' and I said, without hesitation, 'Royal Engineers, sir.' Nice safe job!

Hannaford was sent first to Manchester for officer training. After six months he was commissioned and sent to Clitheroe in Wales to await his posting. His friends all seemed to be getting rather interesting postings, and he awaited news of his own destination.

Each day we looked at the notice board in the officers' mess and there were tabs of paper there. One day one of my friends and I walked in and he pulled out this little slip and it said 'West Indies. Water engineer'. Wartime, West Indies – I thought, well that's not too bad. Within a couple of days there was another slip and this time it was a road engineer for South Africa. Not bad either. A couple of days after that I went up and sure enough my little slip was there. I opened it up and it said: 'You will report to Number 16 Bomb Disposal Company in Cardiff.' Oh dear.

Training had improved considerably over the previous year, as more and more came to be known about the German ordnance they would be facing on a daily basis. Bomb disposal was out of its infancy. Different fuzes such as the 15, 17 and 50 had been identified and the means of neutralizing them was becoming more refined. After an initial spell of 'hands-on' training in Swansea with a more experienced officer, Hannaford was one of the first officers to attend the newly instituted bomb disposal course at Ripon in Yorkshire. It was not long before he was on his way back to Wales to take charge of his own section in Newport.

The first bombs he was sent to deal with were all straightforward 50-kilogram bombs with ordinary impact fuzes. As time went on, Hannaford remembers his feelings towards the job changing in a most unexpected way.

It was rather an odd thing really. At the beginning I had immense confidence. I knew how to deal with it and I wanted to get on with it. I wanted to be a bomb disposal officer. But the strange thing was that the more I did the more nervous I got. The reverse of what you would expect. Towards the end I didn't like the job very much.

Hannaford was becoming more and more aware of the arbitrary nature of the danger he was facing. Stories regularly filtered back about death and injury among his colleagues. He was particularly upset to hear about the death of his mentor in Swansea, caused by a bomb near the General Hospital. He heard of it in a phone call from the section driver, who had been spared only because he had left the officer for the briefest of moments.

It was clear that even the most careful and fastidious of officers could still be caught out, despite recognizing the fuze and knowing exactly what to do. This uncertainty increased yet further the pressures of a pressurized job, yet the prevailing attitude was still one of pragmatic dedication. Lieutenant Bryan Richards was another officer who exemplified this approach. He had come into bomb disposal in 1941 from what was described as a reserved occupation. This meant that his job, as an architect in charge of property belonging to the City of London Corporation, was considered valuable to the war effort and so prevented him being called up. However, when invasion began to seem more and more likely, Richards asked to be allowed to join up, and was commissioned into the Royal Engineers.

He was sent for two weeks' training and 'converted from a civilian to a Royal Engineers Officer' at Chatham. Officers were in very short supply and so at the end of this fortnight, all but one of his intake of officers were posted into bomb disposal. It was on to Melksham in Wiltshire for a week of nominal training in bomb disposal – Richards realized very quickly that his real training would take place on the job. Fortunately he felt suited to it.

> *I realized only afterwards that I fitted the job because it needed care and very careful observation and taking notice of the infor-mation and instructions which one was given. I recognized that the people who had given the instructions knew what they were talking about. Some people thought they could take short cuts. I never did. It was the people who took the short cuts that blew themselves up.*

His cool head and steady hand were never more needed than when he found himself defuzing a bomb at the Yorkshire Grey pub in Eltham, south-east London, in late 1941. It had been an exceptionally busy period for him as he had dealt with twenty-three bombs in just nine days. This bomb had fallen in through a dance hall at the rear of the pub and was given an A2 category. The hall was important because it had been requisitioned as an Army recruiting centre and, as such, held vital records that could not be lost. In addition, it was at the junction of several roads so there had been considerable disruption to traffic as well as hundreds of people evacuated from their homes. At this time all UXBs were left for at least seventy-two hours in case the fuze was a type 17. The safety period having come to an end, Richards was assigned to deal with it.

The digging was completed fairly quickly and the fuze was uncov-ered. However, the ground was gravelly and water kept on filling up the hole and obscuring the bomb. Richards carried on digging himself, unwilling to risk the lives of his men. When eventually he uncovered the bomb he saw that the fuze was indeed a 17. It should have gone off within the designated period but experience had shown that if it had not, then the slightest movement could cause it to detonate. The first thing Richards did was to try and find out if it was ticking by attaching a stethoscope. One of the sappers in his section was at the safe point listening: 'They shouted out, "It's ticking!" I immediately beat a retreat. Then it stopped so I went back to deal with it. There was water in the hole so that had to be got out first before I could do any more. Then the clock restarted.'

Richards had to leave the hole again only to re-enter when the clock stopped. This happened repeatedly, on each occasion the time the clock had left to run was getting shorter. Richards worked continuously for eighteen hours with water rising and being pumped out continuously. It was suspected that the bomb would have a second fuze pocket that would contain the treacherous number 50 anti-handling fuze, but the soft ground made finding it almost impossible: 'It seemed to me that there wasn't going to be a hope of getting the bomb out with the fuzes dealt with, and the only thing that I could do – and it wouldn't be easy – was to put an explosive charge on it and blow the bomb up. I telephoned headquarters and got authority to do that.'

Richards then went back down into the hole and attached the charge. He was in three feet (almost a metre) of muddy water and the risk of becoming trapped was high. Fortunately he was able to climb out of the hole and, using sandbags, he successfully tamped down the force of the explosion. None of the papers was lost and the building received only light damage. Richards's bravery was not to go unrecognized. General Taylor, Director of Bomb Disposal, later commented: 'I consider that this is an outstanding example of cold-blooded courage and determination for which the award of the George Cross would appear appropriate.' As Richards was soon to find out, the recommendation was in part approved.

Somewhat unusually, Richards was then sent to Aldershot on a less demanding mission: to learn about mess procedures at the Army Catering Corps Headquarters. It was here that he received the surprise notification of his decision.

A few months afterwards I was reading the newspaper after lunch in the officers' mess and found that my name was included in a list of people who had been awarded the George Medal. Well, I had not been told that there was anything like this going on so I thought it must be a mistake. I rang the Company and they said, 'Oh no. It isn't a mistake. It is you!' The whole thing came as a complete surprise to me. That bomb had to be dealt with and I was just dealing with it. If one were thinking all the time about what might happen if things went wrong you would never get the job done. You just did what you knew was the right thing to do.

Despite or perhaps because of the dangers they faced, bomb disposal officers grew to have a grudging respect for the technical excellence of the fuzes they were dealing with. Nevertheless, gossip and chat about their work, even among themselves, was positively discouraged. There were posters everywhere warning of the dangers of indiscretion – not least the classic 'Careless Talk Costs Lives'. The maxim extended beyond ordinary soldiers and the general public, far into the upper echelons of government.

Lord Rothschild, whose family had founded an international banking dynasty, was using his global connections working for MI5. He regularly co-ordinated the recovery of fuzes from the Continent through covert means, handing them over for research purposes. His work had given him a great interest in bomb disposal and he enjoyed a close relationship with the scientists at the Ministry of Supply. In February 1942 he approached Dr E. T. Paris asking for information regarding the latest in bomb disposal techniques. He hoped to obtain an outline of basic disposal methods in order that the information could be disseminated among special agents abroad. The request was passed in a memo to the Director of Scientific Research, Dr Gough. Gough's handwritten reply was succinct and illustrated the sensitivity of the information he was being asked to impart:

I fail to see any reason whatever why Lord Rothschild should have such a description. As you are aware, the less put on paper the better and it is foolish to take unnecessary risks. I suggest that unless Rothschild can show powerful reasons, his request be gently but firmly turned down.

As indeed it was: even Lord Rothschild, with his considerable influence and high-level security clearance, was refused information.

Back in the field, this secrecy contributed to the isolation that many officers felt. The daily life for a bomb disposal officer, especially those not in the metropolitan areas, could be extremely lonely. Eric Wakeling remembers that the natural division between the officers and the ranks could sometimes contribute to this problem.

If we didn't turn up for breakfast the only people who were going to miss us were our men and the company commander who had been told that we were blown up. In that respect it was very difficult to live anything other than a very closed personal life. It was because we didn't have anyone to talk to. Yes, you might talk to your sergeant a certain amount, but when the men were off duty they wanted to be down the pub.

There were of course compensations that came with rank. Promotion came quickly for many and although some felt the two pips that denoted the rank of lieutenant was the only reward they did get, for some the headiness of youth combined with power became rather an intoxicating experience. Despite his increasing reservation and nervousness, John Hannaford remembers the job as having an addictive quality.

All of us got so hooked on bomb disposal: it was such an interesting thing. It was dangerous but it was interesting. It wasn't heroic stuff, but you were doing a recognized job. I was a young man about twenty-two years old and all of a sudden I was given this enormous authority, something I had never had in my life before. The police wanted to know who I was, where I was, how

*they could contact me and so on. If a bomb dropped in the
middle of Newport the police would come to me and ask what
areas should be evacuated. This is heady stuff for a young fellow.
I don't think it went to our heads, but it was part of the deal.
You were somebody.*

On one occasion, however, Hannaford had cause to wonder if he
had gone from being somebody to a 'nobody', when he attended an
unexploded bomb near the River Usk in early spring 1942. Following
the usual procedure, a call had come into their company office in
Cardiff to say that a stick of bombs had dropped near a bridge over the
river. Reports estimated that there were one or possibly two UXBs, and
Hannaford set off with his section and the usual six-figure map refer-
ence to undertake a survey of the site. Near a farmhouse they found
the first hole – from its diameter of about 2 feet (60 centimetres),
Hannaford was able to determine that the bomb was probably a 250-
kilogram: not good news. A bomb of this size was big enough to hold
a number 17 fuze which, by virtue of its added clockwork mechanism,
was considerably longer than the 15 fuze. The second hole, nearer the
river, was of a similar size and it was this bomb that he decided should
be excavated first.

After probing the ground and gauging the angle of entry,
Hannaford instructed his men where to dig. After two days he heard
that the bomb's tail fin had been located and he returned to the site.
The tail fins would detach from the bomb as it entered the ground but
the bomb would continue on for some feet. However, the fins did
confirm what Hannaford had first thought: it was a 250-kilogram
bomb. The River Usk was tidal at the point they were working and
when they had excavated to 5 feet (1.5 metres) the incoming water
combined with the gravel beds created a serious problem. It was a
particularly difficult dig and, despite having three miners in the
section, it took nearly a week to locate the bomb. The mixture of
earth and gravel through which they were digging meant that the
timbers kept falling in, and the water continued to rise. Eventually

they spotted the bomb, but it was not long before the water level rose so far as to cover it again.

The solution was to dig a sump that would lower the water in one particular spot; the water would then drain into the depression, leaving the bomb high and dry. Unfortunately the system did not work and, rather like a child digging a hole on the beach, the quicker they dug, the quicker the water came in. It was a frustrating business. The only piece of good news was that the bomb was lying 'sunny side up' with the fuze on top. But the water was rising fast. Two pumps were now called for.

Eventually with two pumps going full blast we were able to get to the point where just the tail end of the bomb and the fuze could be got at. But at this point I wasn't sure if there was another fuze pocket. Eventually with the help of the miners and the other sappers with their pumps I was able to slide a hand down and make quite sure that we were dealing with one fuze.

Hannaford had prepared himself for the possibility of a second fuze pocket containing a 50 fuze designed as an anti-handling device. He now set about dealing with the one fuze – it was a 17. Was there going to be a Zus40 underneath it? The first job was to find out if the fuze was ticking and to do that the magnetic stethoscope was needed.

We had great difficulty with the microphone. We had to place it on the head of the fuze and somebody a hundred yards back would put the earphones on and if they heard any ticking they would let us know. But you can imagine, with the noise of the pumps and the water it was very difficult to establish whether it was ticking.

Hannaford decided to take a gamble. As the bomb had been in the ground for about ten days, he decided to carry on with the defuzing. Eventually he was ready to extract the fuze using the Merrylees fuze extractor, which enabled the fuze to be removed from a remote location. Incorporating a cap which screwed on to the fuze head and a drum above, there was a cord that was fed through a pulley and could be taken back to a safe point 300 yards away. Hannaford thought he would be 'home and dry any minute'. But then, they literally hit a snag.

The cordage suddenly went taut and, no matter what, I could not get this fuze to move any further. So, what to do? Well, I was a bit young, a little bit ambitious perhaps, and I decided to go and have a look see. I went to the hole and looked down. It was difficult to see the fuze because the drum on top of the fuze obscured the view. I thought it was a fairly safe bet to go down the hole and have a look underneath the drum. I could see the fuze was far enough up that had there been a Zus40 underneath it would certainly have blown up. I felt fairly safe with the extractor and found that the fuze was jammed in the fuze pocket. So there was this greeny-grey steel bomb and this bright shiny fuze. I did what I had to do; I got hold of it and lifted it out.

The noise at the base of the hole was deafening with two pumps working at full power. One was a diaphragm pump and the other a centrifugal pump which was operated by compressed air that shrieked 'like a banshee making a hell of a noise'.

Within a flash my world vanished. I was there one moment holding a shiny fuze and the next moment I couldn't see anything. I'm dead. The good news was that it was lightish, cloud-like, and almost celestial. I began to look for my harp and then a voice said, 'Are you all right, sir?'

Hannaford realized he was still very much in this world. The tubing from the compressor had come loose, sending out a very fine white cloud of water spray and momentarily blinding him. Back at the safe point, the lance sergeant had mistaken the mist for steam and, thinking very quickly, had switched off the other pump so creating a sudden and rather shocking silence. As Hannaford came back to himself, he realized he had forgotten to complete a vital part of the sequence: 'I hadn't unscrewed the gaine, which is the end of the fuze and, though tiny, is absolutely lethal. So I took that off and started to climb the ladder. I got halfway up with the fuze in one hand and it fired; a flame about eighteen inches long shot across my face.'

Unbeknown to Hannaford, the clock in the 17 fuze had started ticking and, having reached the end of its pre-set time, had fired the fuze. Poor machining in the clock had meant that the clock had probably stopped just short of firing; like a wristwatch that goes for a few seconds when it is shaken, the jarring that occurred when Hannaford had pulled it out of the fuze pocket had been just enough to set it ticking again. Had he not removed the gaine, the small amount of explosive in the fuze would have been enough to severely injure or even kill him. As it was, he was lucky to escape uninjured.

As mentioned earlier, the fact that the larger and more complex 17 fuze was expensive to produce, and could be used only in bombs of 250-kilograms and more, restricted its use. However, this did not reduce its effectiveness, particularly when it was used in industrialized areas where war production could not be curtailed for any reason. Lionel Meynell was an officer based in Coventry, a key manufacturing city that was to be devastated by ferocious bombing raids. He and a fellow officer dined together one evening and discussed a bomb only recently uncovered and requiring imminent defuzing.

He told me it was fitted with a 17 and that he was going to take it out. It was also fitted with a 50 fuze. I asked him if he could destroy the bomb in situ. The answer was no. It was near a factory. He went out to this bomb to deal with it and it exploded. I had the very disagreeable task of going round with the sergeant and collecting bits of the bodies of the six men who had gone with him. We had the funeral service in Coventry Cathedral about a fortnight before it was destroyed.

Meynell is almost certain that it was not the 17 fuze that had caused the detonation in this instance. It was much more likely to have been the 50, given the force of the explosion and the resultant devastation. Meynell himself was shortly to face his own particular challenge.

Bombs that had had their fuzes removed were fairly inert. Nevertheless, they were usually taken to the 'bomb cemetery', an open piece of ground away from houses, to be exploded. Most bombs were filled with TNT, which had a solid waxy texture, but some were filled with a powdered explosive. Occasionally a bomb containing the powdered filling would fail to explode and, without the solid support of the TNT to hold the fuze pocket in place, it would shear off and drop inside the bomb casing. It was a bomb like this that faced Meynell one day. It was impossible to tell what kind of fuze it was as it had detached and was lying inside the powdered filling. The only option was to take off the base plate and scoop out as much of the powder as possible. The lance-sergeant and section driver helped Meynell in the task but, before they could finish, the bomb exploded.

The driver was killed, while the lance-sergeant and Meynell were severely injured. Amazingly, the two survivors had enough strength to drag the driver to the truck but, before they could attempt to drive away, an ambulance arrived and took them to hospital, where Meynell was to stay for six weeks recovering from his injuries. He remembers the event clearly: 'It was a quarry and it had stones in it. I felt terrific pain in my legs and my back and my ears were gone. One thing that I remember very clearly was that the trench coat I was wearing was all in shreds, just shreds. And the sergeant, he had a hole in his shoulder you could almost see through.'

Meynell was deeply affected by the death of the young driver, who he remembers as a very happy-go-lucky kind of boy who was always smiling. When he returned to 9 Company, John Biggs, the Officer

Commanding, asked him if he wanted to carry on. He did not hesitate in confirming his intention to stay in bomb disposal.

I think my attitude was exactly the same as any other officer in the army: you carried on with what you were doing. It was the same with the fellows who were blown up in the tanks: if they survived they were posted to another unit and back into tanks. Or it was like the RAF pilots who were shot down and rejoined another unit. It was an attitude of mind: we had to win the war.

As Meynell points out, his attitude was by no means unique. 'Do or die' heroism could be seen throughout the armed services particularly in the darkest days of 1940–1 when Hitler was making steady progress and the bombing raids were devastating. It was to be some months before the breakthrough in North Africa turned the course of the war and had Rommel on the run. In the meantime, the home front had to be kept as secure as possible and defeat could not be countenanced.

However, it is perhaps surprising that more men did not want to be moved to other less hazardous companies within the Royal Engineers, given that officially all those who worked in bomb disposal had the option to leave after six months if they wished. (Not that this message reached everybody, it would seem.) It had been felt in the early days of bomb disposal that extended service would result in similar reactions to those seen after the First World War where shell shock, known today as post-traumatic stress disorder, would eventually lead to many being debilitated. A few did leave, but the truth remains that even if everyone had known they had the opportunity to leave after six months, hardly any would have availed themselves of the opportunity. As Meynell readily admits, their almost daily encounters with stressful and dangerous situations were to them definitely no different to anything being faced by others in the armed forces: 'We knew we might be blown up. It was all part of the mental picture you had of what was required of you. It was war. One accepted it. I don't think that you ever overcame the fear or the knowledge that the thing might go up while you were dealing with it, or the men might get killed. You never overcame that.'

For those who were never told of the option of leaving, it has come as something of a revelation. John Hannaford is one of many who discovered only recently that he could have left. But like most, even if he had known, leaving would not have been considered. For Hannaford, it remains an unforgettable, seminal period in his life:

Looking back over my long lifetime, there has been nothing else like it. It's so vivid in my mind now. The strange thing is the ability of the mind to remember voices. The sergeant who called to me at the Usk bomb – I can hear his voice now. And the sappers who were killed – I can hear their voices now. It's very emotive and it is something very, very powerful in my life.

John Hannaford is not alone in remembering the bravery of the sappers who served underneath him. Stuart Archer, promoted to colonel, also pays tribute: 'They might have been bakers or builders or anybody before I took them on. They were thrown into the middle of this. It was they who were the ones doing the digging on top. They sat on the bomb for longer than me. I came in at the end and dealt with the fuze.'

An over-simplification, perhaps, but bomb disposal seen through the eyes of the sappers in the ranks adds yet another dimension to this remarkable story.

3

The sapper's story

Nobody thinks they're not going to go off when they drop on you. When we dug them out, we didn't think they were going to go off. No one mentioned that.

SAPPER ERNEST ACTON

SCOTSMAN HARRY VALLANCE was a stonemason in the town of Lockerbie when war broke out. Not wanting to wait until he was called up, he decided that the Royal Engineers was the Corps in which he could usefully employ the skills he already had, as well as developing new ones. After some basic instruction in fence construction and bridge building – during which time he was billeted in a barracks very overcrowded after the Dunkirk evacuation – he was sent to Swansea.

Vallance and his section arrived with their sergeant one summer evening in 1940 and immediately met the kind of disorganization and lack of preparation that characterized the early stage of the war: 'There was nobody there to meet us and nobody knew where we had to go. The transport officer in association with some welfare unit put us up in the church hall for the evening and told us to use some old curtains as blankets.'

Vallance and his section were attached to the Welsh Regiment for rations but, as well as having nowhere to sleep, they were lacking basic equipment: 'We had no tools, no equipment, nothing. The vehicle was a breakdown lorry requisitioned by the officer. The tools to excavate the bombs we borrowed from Swansea Borough Council. We had picks and shovels from them which they later donated to us to sell when we got our own equipment.'

As described earlier, the work required to make an unexploded bomb safe fell into two parts, broadly speaking: discovering the bomb and then defuzing it. The uncovering of it was left largely to the skills and ingenuity of the sappers, many of whom were skilled tradesmen with experience of joinery, building and even mining. The defuzing, once the bomb was uncovered, was supposed to be done by officers but shortages of trained officers often meant that sections were left alone to complete this task. Harry Vallance was a sapper in one of those sections.

About six or seven o'clock the following morning the officer called us. Somebody had informed him where we were and that there was a bomb in Danigreg Road. This bomb had hit a manhole cover and hadn't penetrated; it was just lying on the ground. We'd never seen one before. I hadn't even seen a picture!

The officer was not with them, but he had given the sergeant a rough description of what he might find and told him to remove the fuze. They found what they assumed to be the fuze and unscrewed it more 'out of curiosity than anything'. Their curiosity could well have cost them their lives – on this occasion, they were lucky. The fuze came out safely and they removed the bomb.

However, in the early months even digging down to the bomb could be extremely hazardous. Finding the bomb would continue to be one of the most difficult aspects of bomb disposal for the duration of the war. The entry hole was merely an indication of where the bomb might be. The angle of entry and type of ground together with underground obstacles such as drainpipes all had a bearing on where the bomb might have ended up and accordingly where the hole should be dug. Harry Vallance explains how the lack of timber needed to shore up the sides of the shaft caused considerable danger:

In sand it might come back to the surface but in clay it would go down as far as 20 feet. We've been down as far as 25 feet. In the early days we had no timber, so we'd just excavate as we thought fit and follow whoever had the most experience. [In clay] you could follow the hole. In sand or soil it was sometimes difficult to follow and you had to keep probing. Once you found it you had to remove the fuze and get it out. If we were suspicious of the excavation collapsing we just used to warn the public around and blow it up.

As shoring became more and more essential to the safe excavation of bombs, any and all materials could be employed: floorboards from bombed houses, old doors – anything that would help support the sides of the hole. As the shaft became deeper it became impossible for the sapper who was digging at the bottom of the hole to throw the earth all the way to the top. These deep excavations required staging platforms to be installed: a 'shelf' was installed above the sapper on to which he threw the excavated earth. Another sapper would in turn throw this earth on to the surface or if necessary to the next stage.

Recruiting offices were opening all over the country. Conscription was not, as yet, in full force, but such was the general feeling that many young men were choosing to volunteer before being called up. In doing so, as Harry Vallance had found, they were more likely to receive a posting of their choice. Ernest Acton – he who had that enlightening exchange with a complacent officer in Chapter 1 – had been in the Territorial Army before the war, and shortly after it started he volunteered to join a field company of the Royal Engineers in Manchester. To his disappointment he was soon told that following the rest of his company to France was out of the question.

He may have been keen, but he was still too young. It was not long, however, before Acton's wartime career was to start its path. The company sergeant major asked him whether he would like to go on a course.

Well, you know, when somebody asks you what you want to do in the Army you've got to be very careful. Then he asked if I could play cricket. Even worse – two questions in one day! I said, well, I am better at bowling. He said, you're just the man to go bomb throwing. My heart sank. I could see myself standing on a slit trench with a bloomin' bomb in my teeth, getting the pin out.

The 'bomb throwing' course was not all it appeared and Acton never did throw a grenade, but he did learn how to blow bombs up. From there he was sent to Sheffield where he was attached to a cavalry regiment and spent his days waiting for bombs to fall. It would appear that the course was not a little lacking in detail. The paucity of information regarding the safe disposal of ordnance became glaringly obvious when Acton went to his first bomb, which was British, having been dropped out of an aeroplane belonging to the Royal Air Force.

The two weeks' training that we had was really just how to deal with bombs that were buried. They didn't know anything about the fuzes. When we went to the RAF bomb, I picked up my notes and it said that if a bomb is buried put on 20 pounds of explosives. So we stuck on umpteen sticks of gelignite. The crater was about four times bigger than it would have been if the bomb had gone off!

Information about fuzes was largely lacking until Acton moved to a regular bomb disposal section in the early summer of 1940. He is still perplexed today about the ignorance surrounding UXBs in the middle of 1940:

I can't understand myself why they hadn't got the fuzes because they had been dropping them in other places. Rotterdam and all these other cities that had been bombed before, you'd have thought they'd have realized that the bomb that doesn't go off is sometimes a bigger menace than the one that does.

Ernest Acton was the senior member of his section, and much of the work that should have been done by the section's officer fell to him. Trained officers were in very short supply; with the infantry regiments needing men for front-line jobs, the services were to have great difficulty in finding enough officers for the home front. It was an experience shared across the country. The shortages were not helped by the high casualty rates. One report covering four weeks in September and October 1940 shows a total of forty-two killed and twenty-one injured. With 3,187 bombs dealt with, the casualty ratio was high.

Cecil Brinton was another sapper who joined up relatively early in June 1940. At twenty-seven years old, he had seen younger men being called up and, by the time of the Dunkirk evacuation, had decided to follow his father's footsteps and join the Royal Engineers. By 15 July Brinton was on a train to Nottingham for his basic training, which included trench building and marching – little of which came in particularly useful when he was sent to Leeds to join a bomb disposal section. On 29 August, Brinton was on his way to the Duke of York's Barracks in London. That night, the Blitz started. For Cecil Brinton and his section baptism was almost literally by fire.

He headed out to the site of his first bomb at Clapham Common with four other sappers and no officer. More worrying was the fact that basic training had omitted bomb disposal from its curriculum completely: 'I was told to dig until we found something, some unidentified object. We didn't know anything about bomb disposal. We had no training whatsoever. We were just told to dig.'

As they were digging, the ack-ack (anti-aircraft) guns around the common scared them half to death. Earlier that day fire from these guns had forced them to dive for cover. It was not too surprising when the 'unidentified object' they had been charged with finding turned out to be an unexploded ack-ack shell – extremely dangerous if hit with a pick or a shovel. Acton and his section were among those who had the good fortune to survive their early experiences working in bomb disposal.

Jack Curtis was another sapper whose first bomb turned out to be a shell. He had originally joined another regiment, and after the Dunkirk evacuation – when the German invasion seemed a serious possibility – he, along with tens of thousands of other soldiers the length and breadth of the country, was confined to barracks in the summer of 1940. Curtis was young and a little restless to say the least, so when the opportunity of escape was offered, he took it. He remembers the distinctive livery on the bomb disposal vehicle that arrived at his barracks:

Passes to get out of the barracks were few and far between. One day a lorry came into the barracks with red painted wings. I asked the driver what it was all about and he said, 'We're bomb disposal.' I asked him what bomb disposal did and he said we dig up unexploded bombs. I had never heard of it.

The driver asked Curtis if he wanted a job.

Anything to get out of this place, were my thoughts. At that moment, Jim Coward the sergeant came out of the offices and I told him. He said right, pack your kit, and within the hour I was on the back of a lorry heading towards Dartford. I was at home that night, sleeping at home – the first time I had done that for a long, long time.

So keen was Curtis to get out of the barracks that he had not given any thought to what might lie ahead. To him the job involved 'exposing a bomb in the ground and pulling it out'. The issues surrounding fuzes and booby-traps were as yet unknown to him. It had not even occurred to him that a bomb might penetrate deep into the ground. To Jack Curtis, bomb disposal was a means of being somewhere near home. He was billeted in a house near the grounds of Dartford Football Club. The pitch was used to store dead bomb cases. Like Cecil Brinton, Curtis found training was non-existent: 'There was no training. You just went out on the job and you more or less sort of picked up what lads who were already in the bomb disposal section told you.'

Curtis's first job was to recover a 'missile' at Northfleet Church. When he and his fellow sapper arrived they saw the damage to the roof and the corresponding hole in the floor of the church. The floor was very hard and, without the benefit of a pneumatic drill, the going was tough. After 3 feet (nearly a metre) of digging, an ack-ack shell was uncovered. With the shell out of the ground, the next challenge was to get back to barracks – with the shell. Curtis was charged with finding a suitable mode of transport. He stopped the first lorry that passed, climbed into the cab and put the shell between his knees. Had he realized that the lorry belonged to the British Oxygen Company and was laden with tanks, he might have waited for the next vehicle. As it was, the driver – made slightly less nervous by being assured the shell was dead – took him and his load to Dartford, to be met by section sergeant Jim Coward.

When Coward realized that what had been brought back was in fact an unexploded shell, he was less than pleased. Now the driver's suspicions were aroused. When he learnt the true situation, he was quickly back in his cab. 'Shall we say he got out of the football ground very, very quick and that's the last we saw of him!' remembers Curtis.

But not all incidents Jack Curtis dealt with had such a fortunate outcome. He had been in bomb disposal for only a few weeks when he was to come face to face with tragedy, and one that but for a few feet might have claimed his life. He and a fellow sapper called Nixon were sent to uncover a bomb that had fallen through a rockery behind the surgeon's house at the Joyce Green Hospital near Dartford. It was a hot summer day when he and Nixon began to dig, and they took it in turns

in the ever deepening hole. Curtis had cultivated a friendly relationship with the hospital and their tiring work and resultant thirst was
rewarded with jugs of water whenever they wanted. By about midday
on the second day of digging they had uncovered the bomb, and Curtis
was dispatched for refreshments.

*I must have got about fifteen yards from the thing and away she
went. I got knocked flat and as I looked up I could see all the
debris. I thought what goes up must come down so I made a bolt
for the garden shed and dived underneath the bench. Down
came the debris and it came through the roof. Then it went all
quiet, deathly quiet. I went looking for [Nixon]... He wasn't
there. They never found him.*

Whether Nixon had hit the fuze or tried to remove it himself, or
whether it had been a type of fuze as yet unfamiliar to the Royal
Engineers, will never be known. The explosion left Curtis completely
deaf for a few days and even today he still has recurrent bouts of
tinnitus (ringing in the ears). At the time, he had two days off work
before he returned to Dartford. Then for a few days he worked in the
cookhouse. The attitude of the 'lads' to his lucky escape was mixed:
'Some of the lads thought I was an omen – some thought I was good,
some thought I was bad. If they went with me, it had already
happened to me so perhaps it wouldn't happen again. Others thought,
well, if it's happened to him once, it might happen again.'

It was not long before Curtis returned to full bomb disposal duties.
There was no time to dwell on trauma, and Curtis's experiences were
by no means unusual. In blitz-torn central London, Cecil Brinton's
section was not having an easy time of it either. As a lance sergeant he
lost the majority of two sections on different occasions, both of which
spared him through luck rather than judgement. The first was at an
incident in Croydon where there were two UXBs to be uncovered and
defuzed – one in a garden and the other in a school playground.
Brinton had just left part of his section digging at the school site to

check on the men at the other site when he heard an explosion. It claimed the lives of many friends, but the next day the men were replaced and the job went on.

The second incident a few weeks later killed among others the 21-year-old officer in charge of Brinton's section. Brinton remembers feeling a little fatherly when he had first met the young man who was in charge of him and his men. They had gone to deal with a bomb that had not penetrated the ground. The bomb was lying in such a way that the fuze head was angled downwards, towards the ground.

We were both nervous, of course. He put the extractor in, tied a bit of string to the ring on it and we went back to get out of sight. Just as we got back the fuze dropped out on its own! The officer said, 'Oh, I do feel like such a fool.' I looked at him and I must have been feeling like Methuselah at the time, because I said to him, it's better to be a live coward than a dead hero.

Brinton is not sure whether the officer took any notice but it was not long before his section was digging up a bomb in another built-up area. The bomb had hit the gutter and passed through an iron water main and in so doing had damaged the fuze. The ARP warden had taken round a hat and it was nearly filled with coins. It was not uncommon for the public to show their appreciation for the work of the bomb disposal sections in this way. The hundreds of people who had been evacuated were all anxious to get back to their homes, but were grateful for the work the sappers were doing.

The corporal in charge of the work decided that, as the bomb did not require any digging, the bomb could be taken away. It was loaded into the truck and taken back to the barracks, where the tired and hungry men ate their evening meal. Brinton returned to the barracks late that day and remembers hearing about what happened next.

The section officer came in and saw this bomb in the back of the truck with the fuze still in it. It looked as if it didn't present any danger because of the state of it. But he decided it couldn't be left in the barracks as it might blow up. We used to take [the bombs] to Regent's Park and so they set off. There was about eight of them on this truck and the driver asked to be excused because he had a date with his girlfriend. So the officer drove the truck himself. They got to somewhere in the vicinity of Madame Tussaud's and this bomb exploded. It blew the lot to pieces. They wanted to go and dump the bomb and have a few drinks on the way back. I would probably have joined them if I'd been there.

Harry Vallance was to have a similar experience in Swansea. He had never become used to seeing the devastation that bombing brought, but he did manage to harden himself to certain things he saw. They are, however, still vivid in his memory. During his time in bomb disposal six of his fellow comrades were to lose their lives in one incident – one in which Vallance too would have been killed if he had not been working late into the night at Pembroke Dock: 'My unit was supposed to be on duty that evening but because we had been away for three days and been out all the time and had no rest, the others said it wasn't right that we should go. So they went and we had a night's sleep.'

The following morning after their night's rest, Vallance's section got a call to attend an unexploded bomb at a nearby prison, which was only a short distance from where the part of his section that had gone out the night before was working.

We went there the following morning and while we were there, we heard this explosion. We guessed what had happened. We went flying round there and there were six of our chaps – gone. The officer who was there at the time, he was staggering about with his ears bleeding and he was shell-shocked. The sergeant didn't know what had happened to them. The staff sergeant and the lance sergeant were killed too.

The Red Cross and an ambulance unit had been nearby and had done what they could. Some bodies had been removed by the time Vallance arrived. Other body parts were being collected. Vallance and his fellow sappers were required to identify the bodies as best they could. Swansea's mortuaries were very full and temporary facilities were made available in village and school halls. He will never forget the sights he saw that day: 'I think it was one of the worst sights I ever saw in bomb disposal. The bodies were stacked the way you would stack wood – like a pyramid. They weren't even washed. They were a dreadful sight because they mostly turned black and they were bleeding.'

Efforts were always made to give such victims a dignified funeral, but the nature of their injuries often entailed special measures.

The coffins of these six chaps were sealed and not to be opened. They were only filled with sand, in my opinion. The smallest chap had the heaviest coffin; the largest chap, the staff sergeant, had the lightest coffin. I think that upset some for some time. Some chaps did give in, you know. They were transferred after these sights.

Cecil Brinton also saw many of his own men blown to pieces, picking up their broken bodies so that there was something for their relatives to bury. But there is one sight that still haunts him today, the memory of sixty years ago as raw and real as if it happened yesterday. Early one morning his section got a call to attend a UXB in a street in London. The ARP had erected barricades at the end of the street by the time they arrived and it was obvious that people were anxious to return to their homes following the previous night's raid. One woman seemed particularly agitated. Brinton was sent to the house where the bomb had fallen. He found the bomb on the ground floor, removed the fuze and ordered his men to take the bomb to the truck before going upstairs to check the damage. It was then that the reason for the lady's extreme state of anxiety became apparent.

This lady had left her baby in a cot in the bedroom. The bomb had gone through the roof right into the cot. It smashed the cot and the baby to pieces. I got a pillowcase and picked up what I could of the baby. I put it in the pillowcase and left it there. I told the ARP warden and the policemen what I had done and said I couldn't face the mother. I know what they mean by trauma. It can have a lasting effect.

Cecil Brinton was one of the men in bomb disposal who were not told about the provision of transferring out after six months; neither were Harry Vallance and Ernest Acton. Unsurprisingly, none of them when asked now would have left even if they had known there was a choice – even when, as was often the case, there was no officer to actually defuze a bomb and the job fell to a sapper.

Around this time, the officer attached to Cecil Brinton's section had been killed and there was a hiatus before the position was filled. During this time, Brinton carried out the duties of the officer unaware of the danger he was facing.

I didn't know that there were number 15s, 17s, 50s. I knew later, but at that time I had no idea. I presumed the officer had known but when he was killed I had to carry on and take his place. It was many weeks before we had a replacement officer and our section was made up to strength again. I was taking out these fuzes and didn't have any idea, any idea what to expect. I must have had a guardian angel or something. I remember one bomb I went to and all I had was a key because the stethoscope had disappeared and the two-pin plug had been discarded because they thought it was booby-trapped. So I went down and undid the fuze and took it out. I had no idea what I was doing and many people got killed just doing that.

On another occasion Brinton attended a bomb and realized he had forgotten the key required to unlock the fuze in its pocket only when it was too late: 'I found a rusty four-inch nail in the truck and a heavy spanner, and just punched around it and got it out. It just shows you that we were taking our lives in our own hands really.'

If Cecil Brinton had been an officer he would have received the bulletins sent out with great regularity from the Inspectorate of Fortifications and Bomb Disposal. Being without an officer, his section had not heard of the recent discoveries made in Wales by Lieutenant Stuart Archer. Instead, Brinton was reduced to gleaning information as and when anyone decided to share it. There was one man to whom he credits the vast majority of his knowledge – a remarkable and to some notorious figure: the Earl of Suffolk and Berkshire.

Charles Henry George Howard, the 20th Earl of Suffolk and 13th Earl of Berkshire, had always been a colourful character blessed with charisma, charm and good looks. As a young man, 'Wild Jack' Howard travelled to Australia and found work as a sheep farmer before returning to be commissioned into the Scots Guards. However, his army career was cut short by rheumatic fever, and he was invalided out of the regiment – whereupon he studied for a bachelor's degree in science. On the outbreak of war, Lord Suffolk immediately applied to rejoin his regiment, only to be bitterly disappointed that the long-term effects of rheumatic fever made it impossible for him to return to active service.

He was resolved to be of service to his country, and through his society contacts obtained a position as the personal representative in France of the Director of Scientific Research, Dr H. J. Gough. The directorate came under the auspices of the Ministry of Supply and was responsible for co-ordinating all industrial developments at the time. In this most perilous of times for the Allies, the pooling of information regarding industry was of paramount importance. Lord Suffolk returned to London only after the fall of France, arriving unshaven and sleep-deprived on the steps of the Ministry carrying two large suitcases. Bureaucracy demanded that he fill in a form stating his name and reason for his visit. On this he penned two words – 'Suffolk' and 'diamonds'. The doorman is famously reported to have said that it was his name that was required not his address.

The suitcases were filled with industrial grade diamonds for use in industrial processing – crucial to the Allied war effort. Allowing them to fall into Nazi hands had not been an option for Lord Suffolk. But he had returned with more than diamonds. Having requisitioned a British steamer in Bordeaux, he had also brought back a large group of French scientists whom he billeted in luxury hotels around the capital. However, the most precious cargo of all was also in Suffolk's possession: heavy water, several canisters of it. For a significant period of the war this material, which was essential in the development of the atom bomb, was kept in the same vault as the crown jewels at Windsor Castle, in the strictest secrecy. Not even Lord Suffolk knew where it had been taken; only four people were privy to the information: Lord Wigram, Mr O. F. Morshead (the Windsor Castle librarian), Dr Gough and King George.

After all this excitement, Britain seemed dull by comparison until a chance visit to Dr Gough at the Ministry of Supply set Lord Suffolk out on what was to be his most daring venture yet: the world of bomb disposal. His health had prevented him going on active service but with characteristic disregard for rules and regulations, he bought himself a large van and kitted it out with the necessary equipment to investigate methods of defuzing unexploded bombs. His high level connections aided his maverick approach and eventually a small team of soldiers was seconded to him to help him with his work. His men adored working with the Earl and it was common for him to take them to Kempinski's, a smart London restaurant in Piccadilly Circus where he had a table permanently reserved in his name. Quite what the other regular patrons made of this dirty and dishevelled bunch goes unrecorded by history.

The same government connections also seemed to help him circumvent normal procedures: not only did he have his own research facility and a steady stream of bombs upon which to experiment in Richmond Park, it was also quite common for a section of Royal Engineers to arrive at their designated bombsite to find the Earl at the bottom of a newly dug hole having beaten them to it. When he did not manage to beat them to the bomb, he was still a regular visitor to bombsites all over the south-east. He would arrive wearing his signature plus-fours and smoking a cigarette through a very long holder to take a keen interest in what was going on. Former sapper Cecil Brinton remembers well the first conversation he had with Lord Suffolk, following an extremely lucky fuze extraction.

I remember going to a place in Coulsdon or somewhere in that area. I was digging a bomb and we had had to timber the hole because the ground was unstable, unlike the clay we were used to. When I got down to it there were two fuzes: a 17 and a 50. I didn't know at the time so I just took them out. I took them out and climbed up the ladder and there was the Earl of Suffolk at the top. He congratulated me on the timbering and I handed him the two fuzes. He looked at them and asked me if I knew what they were. I was a lance-sergeant then and I said, 'Yes, they are the fuzes I have just taken out of the bomb.' He said, 'Well, lad, you'll see one is longer than the other. The longest one has a clockwork mechanism on the end.'

That was the first time I had heard that there could be a delayed action fuze. Previous to that I had taken a couple of bombs to him in Regent's Park, but I had never spoken to him till then. After that, every time I went to take a bomb to him he recognized me and we became quite friendly. I learnt more from him at that time about bomb disposal than I ever had. He taught me practically everything there was to know at the time. Whether that was useful or not I don't know. Up until then I would just go and take the fuzes out, whereas probably the next time I'd think twice before I tackled them!

The Earl's charisma inspired devotion in other quarters too. Recording equipment was in short supply and, as it was essential to make accurate records of the procedures and experiments the Earl was undertaking, the services of a secretary were required. Miss Eileen

Morden, who was twenty-seven years of age and had worked for Lord Suffolk in France, volunteered for the job. The Earl's van also required a driver, and Lord Suffolk recruited an elderly man by the name of Fred Hards, who was a skilled mechanic and handyman too. Together, Lord Suffolk, Miss Morden and Fred Hards were known as the Holy Trinity.

Miss Morden took down the Earl's notes in shorthand and had to be close enough to him to hear what he was saying. As such, she was usually much closer than normal regulations allowed. No officer worth his salt would allow one of his men in such close proximity when he was removing a fuze. But such trifling matters failed to make Lord Suffolk change his way of working. Ernest Acton remembers being among top ranking military personnel at a demonstration of a bomb-defuzing technique in Richmond Park that involved chemically burning a hole in the bomb case and burning out the explosive.

I had heard of him and the people that he had drafted to him and that he had done a lot of good work. I think he was quite respected by people like myself. [The section officer] Lieutenant Gosmark came in and said the Earl of Suffolk has got a new idea of tackling these bombs so that you won't have to defuze them. Some of them you couldn't get the fuze out. He had this idea that you could burn it out, you see. I said that it sounded interesting. So he said that we would go tomorrow morning to some common. Old Gosmark was all dressed up in his service dress with his belt and everything so I went and got mine, polished my buttons and off we went.

We got to the common and well, I've never seen so many red tabs. There were all sorts of people there: generals and staff officers, all sorts and we were all looking round this trench. It was only a small trench and in the bottom the Earl of Suffolk had this bomb. He had the filler cap off the end and it was at an angle of about sixty degrees. On top of it he had this earthenware crucible on a little frame. He said, 'I am now going to ignite this and it will set the whole thing going. It will drip onto

the bomb; make a hole in it and the explosive will burn. When
it is burnt out, all we will be left with is a fuze pocket and that's
easy to deal with. We can take it away, no problem.' I thought
that was a bit funny because it would still leave the picric acid
pellets in the fuze!

So anyway, he lit it and we were all standing around looking
knowledgeable. It burns through and the explosive filling started
to burn. Smoke came out the back of this thing and after a bit it
got to look like a rocket and it started roaring! All of a sudden,
as if someone had told them to, everyone turned and ran –
generals, red tabs, everybody – and at some point we all fell on
the ground and it went off! It was incredible, just like it had all
been planned. Everybody got up, walked off and went home.
Nobody said a word. Lord Suffolk was a right case. A very brave
man though.

Lord Suffolk was not without his critics. His apparent disregard for
the safety of those around him was anathema to the officers of the
Royal Engineers. The regulations were clear: only those who were
absolutely necessary should be in the vicinity when defuzing was
taking place. It was very rare indeed for there to be any more than one
person anywhere near the bomb after it had been uncovered.

In May 1941, Lord Suffolk had just returned from a weekend at his
family home, Charlton Park in Wiltshire, which he had turned into a
convalescent home for injured soldiers. Monday was spent searching
for suitable fuzes on which to experiment. It led him to Erith Marshes,
where an old bomb was lying rusted and abandoned. 'Old Faithful' had
been scrawled along the bomb casing. Dr Gough visited him that
morning to watch him work on what he too thought was a 'safe' bomb.
By the time he returned to London the news was through: Lord
Suffolk, Miss Morden and Fred Hards had all been killed. The Holy
Trinity was no more.

Lord Suffolk had done things his own way and arguably, as civilians,
Miss Morden and Fred Hards were both free to walk away: they were

not under 'orders' to do anything – but reports of the time allude to the passionate loyalty engendered in those around Lord Suffolk. A number of other military personnel were killed and injured in this incident but, despite the tragedy, there can be little doubt that Lord Suffolk adhered to the notion of a greater good. He was posthumously awarded the George Cross for his bravery in France and in bomb disposal. Among other things, his experiments had led to the development of a cutting tool used to remove the Zus40 anti-withdrawal device that plagued bomb disposal officers during 1940 and beyond. Miss Morden and Fred Hards both posthumously received the King's Commendation for brave conduct.

Harold Macmillan was to write of Lord Suffolk in his book *The Blast of War* in 1967: 'I have had the good fortune in my life to meet many gallant officers and brave men but I have never known such a remarkable combination in a single man of courage, expert knowledge and indefinable charm.'

4

Conflict and conscience

We are Fred Karno's army
We are the NCC
We do not carry rifles,
What bloomin' use are we?
We're Christians, cranks and bolshies,
We're an assorted lot,
Our major doesn't like us,
He thinks we should be shot!

For many people involved in bomb disposal, there was an almost spiritual nature to the work they were doing. Uncovering a bomb was not to be rushed, and the act of defuzing it required a strict methodology that for some took on the characteristics of a religious rite, such was the care, precision and faith involved in finishing the task correctly. For others who had an anti-war stance, the philosophy behind neutralizing a weapon designed to kill people allowed them an ideological position from which to enter the war. This chapter examines the way in which two men – very different in themselves but with equally strong convictions – integrated their beliefs into their work in bomb disposal.

Early in the war, the shortage of manpower in bomb disposal became a significant problem. The Royal Engineers were involved in more than bomb disposal work, and as a Corps they were stretched to the limit. Fit and able men, particularly those with the skills required to dig for and defuze bombs, were in short supply and were more often than not sent to theatres of war far away from the home front. Prioritizing the distribution of soldiers became a difficult job. There was, however, one 'regiment' of able-bodied men for whom bomb disposal was to be a most suitable occupation. These were the men of the Non-Combatant Corps whose religious or political beliefs had led them to become conscientious objectors.

The Non-Combatant Corps (NCC) had existed during the First World War and was re-formed in April 1940. It consisted of fourteen companies numbering more than 6,000 men at its peak, and was designed to be integral to aspects of the war effort excluding those areas that required the handling of weapons. Those who wished to be registered as conscientious objectors had to appear before a tribunal, which ruled on their sincerity and honesty – not an easy job. For many it was specifically this war and its aims that were wrong. For others, often known as 'absolutes', any armed conflict regardless of the reasoning could never be countenanced. There were also those for whom the war against Nazi Germany seemed just and proper but who thought the taking of human life themselves unimaginable.

As a fifteen-year-old, Christopher Wren had been deeply moved by the plight of the Spanish people during the Civil War in the mid 1930s, and had even considered leaving school to work as a stretcher-bearer. But it was on his trip to Germany three weeks before the Nazis invaded Poland that the reality of what war would mean really hit him: 'This was going to be a different kind of war and it certainly was. I was right about that. People suffered who had never suffered before, as we were to see in the Blitz. It wasn't simply front lines facing each other; it was women and children being bombed. That affected me greatly.'

As war looked imminent in Europe, Wren found his religious and political beliefs galvanized by the influence of the veteran pacifist Fenner Brockway, the socialist Keir Hardie, principal founder of the Labour Party, and his own family history. In the early years of the war, living with his widowed father in Hammersmith, he was a determined pacifist.

> *My father had very strong views after the [First World] War and so did my godfather. Both were similar in that they felt very disillusioned by it all. The 'homes fit for heroes' and so on didn't come about. But in 1933 my father changed completely. He wasn't anti-war any more, but I still felt I was a pacifist. As time went on they said to me, 'What's it going to be?' Meaning, are you going to volunteer for the RAF or are you going to register as a conscientious objector? They didn't see any middle way. I told them, 'It's within you.' I couldn't explain it to them. I thought I couldn't possibly join the RAF in that crusade. I just felt I wasn't made that way.*
>
> *I didn't feel that it was necessary to go to the Bible to believe in anything particular. You must think it from within; you must be conscientious.*

Many of those who appeared before the tribunal may have been unwilling to bear arms but did wish to help nurse those who had been injured; many applied to the Royal Army Medical Corps. However, as the RAMC became flooded with conscientious objectors, morale among those who did not share their ideology suffered. Added to this was the fact that, strictly speaking, the RAMC was an armed regiment. If required, those who served in it had to be prepared to defend their patients and themselves by use of force. (The only regiment of the British Army that was wholly non-combatant was the Royal Army Chaplains' Department.) As such, registered conscientious objectors who were posted to it were excused guard duty and parades. Naturally, this led to further resentment and in time a decision was made to post to the RAMC only those conscientious objectors with specialist qualifications such as radiologists or radiographers. Officially, the reason given was that the Medical Corps was full. But the popular press, which was beginning to question the effectiveness of a corps composed of 'lily-livered conchies', had picked up tensions between the conscientious objectors and the rest of the corps. So on 24 April 1940 the War Office announced the re-formation of the Non-Combatant Corps.

In November 1940 the Director of Bomb Disposal, General Taylor, agreed to accept NCC volunteers. For reasons of morale, it was decided that the proportion was limited to one-eighth of the total number working on bomb disposal at the time. Eventually over 350 Non-Combatant Corps volunteered to work alongside regular Royal Engineers in bomb disposal, a figure considerably less than the quota permitted.

For Christopher Wren and his best friend Charles Parish it was the events of June 1940 that helped convince them that their position as 'absolute' conscientious objectors had to change. As France fell to Nazi occupation, Britain found its troops faced with slaughter as they retreated towards the Channel to be rescued by a flotilla of ships and boats of every shape and size. What became known simply as 'Dunkirk' had a profound effect on the two young idealists:

We were 'absolute' when the war came and carried on that way until Dunkirk. Both of us were overcome by these pictures. We couldn't just stand here and let it happen. Women and children – just let them be open to somebody firing at them, letting them drop and do nothing about it! We were prepared to go and help – on the beaches, stretcher bearing, first aid, and anything that was needed to save life. Germans as well – I should say that.

Non-Combatant Corps basic training took place at Ilfracombe in Devon. It consisted of large amounts of army drill on the promenade (minus weapons, of course). It lasted for four or five days during which time the complex job of handling a pick and shovel was demonstrated at considerable length. Wren's first job as a soldier in the NCC was being seconded to the Pioneer Corps working in forestry, and it was here that he heard about the possibility of volunteering for bomb disposal.

There were from time to time opportunities to volunteer for bomb disposal and once, when it came up, I thought that would be very good: to destroy armaments and at the same time protect people. Both aspects seemed to fit with why I had become non-combatant. The training was minimal. We went to Chester and were under canvas on the racecourse. We met the Royal Engineers there and they were good to us. We had better food than we had had before. Then they told us we would be going to London because there was more to be done down there and so I was sent to Bromley. A few weeks after that we were sent to Chelsea Barracks for real training. We really enjoyed that. It was with the REs and everything was enjoyable. No prejudice at all, not at all.

Nobody in the NCC was forced to go into bomb disposal. Unlike the vast majority of soldiers who found themselves doing this work, they were there by choice. By this time many of the soldiers in the Royal Engineers had been conscripted and Wren remembers the value that his volunteer status brought to what might otherwise have been a very hostile working environment.

With the Royal Engineers we didn't even trouble to talk about war aims or things like that. That wasn't what worried us. The bombs worried us and we got on with it. We were billeted with the Pioneer Corps and that was a sad thing for the NCC – or what we called for a joke the Norwegian Camel Corps! The Pioneers couldn't conceive of what we were thinking about. There were a lot of misconceptions and trouble from time to time. The exceptions among the Pioneer Corps were the people who had volunteered – old soldiers who had a string of medals. They would say to the others who were trying to badger us, 'Don't forget. [The conscientious objectors] did what they wanted to do. You waited for conscription.' Corporal Baker was one in particular who was always saying

that when these silly arguments came up as to what cowards
we were.

But such respect was not to be given to all those who were in the
Non-Combatant Corps. At its worst, the abuse became physical and,
as with all bullying, it was the weakest who made the easiest of
targets. Christopher Wren is still angry when he remembers the treat-
ment he believes his friend Titch Foster received at the hands of the
Pioneer Corps.

He was with me on the bunk above me in bomb disposal.
Originally he went in as an absolute objector and along with a
number of others was physically abused. He was set about by a
number of non-commissioned officers. At one time they had a
couple of boxers on the staff and I think one of them was trying
to hit him in the solar plexus to make him say that he would take
on non-combatant duties. But Titch must have turned. It sounds
impossible in the British Army but he suffered very bad injury to
his back, liver and kidney. He would come in every now and
again, and would say he was going sick. He had maybe one, two
or three appointments on sick parade and on the last of his sick
parades the sergeant major who was, I am sorry to say, from the
Pioneer Corps, ordered him off. Well, unfortunately for the
sergeant major, Titch died.

Later that day the 'conchies' were called out on to parade. The
major wanted to quell the rumours that were flying around concerning
Titch's death.

He gave a lecture and said that there were rumourmongers
among us who knew nothing about the case and the talk had
to stop. Afterwards, I went up to him and said that I was a
'rumourmonger'; I knew Titch all the time I had worked in
bomb disposal, he slept on the bunk above me and he was not

*a malingerer. He had been killed. I wrote to Fenner [Brockway],
the Board of Conscientious Objectors and Titch's mother
saying what a fine fellow he was.*

Although Wren did all he could to alert the authorities to the plight
of Titch and those like him, to the best of his knowledge nobody was
ever held to account for the death of his young friend.

Mercifully, acceptance by the Royal Engineers was not so difficult. Certainly, Christopher Wren has nothing but praise for the way
he was treated by them, and even went on to play for their
regimental football team. While it was his political rather than his
religious beliefs that were the basis for his decision to be a conscientious objector, there were many for whom their faith prevented
them carrying arms. However, on occasion it was their faith that
brought them respect. Harry Vallance remembers working with one
conscientious objector in Wales.

*Some of them were genuine and like everything else, some were
pulling a fast one, but you could pick them out. We didn't have
many [conscientious objectors] until the latter stages and the
majority of them would do anything you asked them to, but they
wouldn't carry arms. Well, we used to have some wild nights, you
know, celebrating and a drink too many at times. We'd been out
one Friday night and came to the communal hut. We were a bit
merry, some of us. The conscientious objector in our section was
a country lad. He had been out with us. The lads used to tease
him, give him a bit of a rough time, but he always stood up to it.*

*This night, when we got in the barracks he took his shoes off
and he knelt beside his bed and prayed. These other lads that
had come in with him stood back. I think they were aghast, and
they just stared at him till he finished. One of them walked up,
shook his hand and said, 'I admire you for being so brave and
praying in front of this gang.' You see, he had asked that his
comrades be spared; make sure nothing happened to them. I*

think that's what touched them, because they heard him say it. Anyway, he got up, shook hands with the others and after that you couldn't separate them. They were wonderful comrades.

Although approval for the Non-Combatant Corps to be used in bomb disposal had been given by General Taylor in November 1940, it was not until March 1941 that they were fully incorporated. While formal training had improved by this time, Christopher Wren found that imitating the sappers was the easiest way to learn.

Naturally, you are very hesitant. You didn't want to do the wrong thing. But I always found it best to look at an RE and see what he was doing and try to do the same. Or, if he wanted something like planks, get them to him. I didn't wait for an order; I just got on and did it. Generally that was the way. All you could do was be as useful as you could possibly be to the Royal Engineers. You couldn't take over from them. They were all skilled people. I'm not a great handyman but I have got strength and they liked that. I could bash about a bit, hardly like a 'conchie'!

Wren remembers one encounter with a bomb where the attention to detail of a 'conchie' saved quite a few lives. This involved the particular danger of what was called a camouflet: that is, when a bomb had penetrated the ground to some considerable depth before exploding, leaving the surface intact but creating an underground cavern filled with carbon monoxide. The sappers would dig down, expecting to find a bomb, but when they had dug down far enough, the roof of the cavern that had been created would eventually collapse under their weight, with instant death inevitable. The procedure for checking for camouflets involved sticking a metal probe into the ground after every few feet of digging. Sometimes, if the bottom of the shaft had filled with water, bubbles would be seen and a quick exit was essential. In addition, the sappers were supposed to wear harnesses attached to a fixed point at the top of the shaft, but this safety measure was not

Above: The eccentric Lord Suffolk observes an experiment. His loyal companions, Fred Hards and Eileen Morden, can be seen by his van. *(Mr Bartleson)*

Below: Life carries on in Sidcup, Kent. The danger sign was a common sight all over Britain during the Second World War. *(Topham Picturepoint)*

DANGER
UNEXPLODED
BOMB

Above: Major John Hudson holds a bottle of liquid oxygen at the site of the first bomb found with a Y fuze, in January 1943. *(John Hudson)*

Below: By February 1943, Hudson had designed a safe container to hold the liquid oxygen when dealing with the Y fuzes, to prevent men being burnt. *(John Hudson)*

Above left: Two sappers from No. 8 Section, 16 BD Co. moving a bomb load in Wales, 1942.
Above right: Complex wooden shoring was essential to prevent shafts falling in on the sappers.
Below left: Lieutenant John Hannaford cautiously probes for a bomb as his sergeant looks on.
Below right: 16 BD Co. practise tieing knots during training in Glamorgan, 1942. *(all John Hannaford)*

Above:
'Butterfly' bombs (SD2s) had wings designed so that they floated down to earth. They were extremely difficult to find and could kill if moved or touched. *(Eric Wakeling)*

Right:
Eric Wakeling *(left)* who spent six weeks dealing with butterfly bombs in Grimsby in the summer of 1943, was only twenty years old when he first defuzed a bomb. *(Eric Wakeling)*

Above: Conscientious objectors could volunteer for bomb disposal. Christopher Wren *(right)* worked in bomb disposal as a member of the Non-Combatant Corps. *(Christopher Wren)*

Below: Sapper Harry Vallance *(front)* with colleagues and two empty bomb cases at Kilvey Quarry near Swansea, 1940. *(Henry Vallance)*

Above: The inventor of the electric fuze, Herbert Erich Ruehlemann *(standing by the post on the right)* at a test site in Reichlin, Germany. *(Elga La Pine)*

Below: Ruehlemann *(second left)* was in close contact with many high-ranking Nazis, including the First World War flying ace and bombing strategist, General Udet. *(Elga La Pine)*

General Ernst Marquard *(left)* was the key decision maker for Luftwaffe bombing strategy. He is pictured here with Herman Goerring *(right)*, Commander of the Luftwaffe. *(Dirk A. Marquard)*

Above left: The Ministry of Supply's Dr H. J. Gough *(second right)* talks to members of the unexploded bomb committee, which comprised top scientists from all over Britain and allied Europe. *(Hulton Getty)*

Above right: Colonel Stuart Archer who removed the first ticking 17 fuze with a Zus40 anti-withdrawal device in a bomb next to a burning oil tank. *(Stuart Archer)*

Below: 69 Section RE proudly display their latest finds in Coventry. Major Lionel Meynell who was severely injured soon after, stands far right. *(Lionel Meynell)*

entirely compatible with efficient digging and, tragically, fatalities did occur, although not in this specific incident.

Up by Crystal Palace there were three camouflets in a row and it was a Born Again Christian who was probing, doing everything properly, with his harness on, and the bubbles started to come up. Now the rules were very clear: if someone fell into a camouflet and he hadn't got a harness on, you left him there. Nobody played any heroics trying to get him out. He was gone and there was no use adding to the total.

Nevertheless, despite the dangers that faced sappers and 'conchies' alike, the accusations of cowardice from the public were frequent, as Wren says: 'If they saw your NCC badge and someone asked what it was, I would say, "Non-Combatant Corps." You know what they are thinking so I would say I was a coward, straightaway! Then sometimes they would see the bomb flash here and they wouldn't know what to make of it all. I would just leave it.'

Wren is the first to admit that not only was he treated with respect by the Royal Engineers throughout his time in bomb disposal, but that he also appreciates the system that allowed him and other conscientious objectors to take such a stance during one of the most bloody conflicts in history.

Our way of life, through our own Parliament, is exceptional. Even when we are on the knife-edge of defeat, we still allow people to register as conscientious objectors. I have already said that some were badly treated but the rest of us, hundreds of us, were well treated in a way that you couldn't take exception to at all. What was strange was that by having this system, we were able to get people to volunteer for jobs like bomb disposal. We were able to use the 'conchies' to do that and we willingly did it. So there was something to be said for our 'cowardice' – if that's the word.

There were many for whom their faith was no barrier to being on active service during the Second World War. Bryan Richards, who as we saw in Chapter 2 defuzed the bomb in the Yorkshire Grey pub in Eltham, felt his faith helped in his work.

I was a Christian and still am. I think war is very stupid and wicked, but I think we have to live with people as they are and not as we think they ought to be. It was obvious to anybody in June 1940 that it was extremely likely that armed Germans would arrive in this country and deal with us in the same way as the other countries they had invaded and controlled. The only way of stopping that was to fight them. That didn't seem to me to be in any way inconsistent with my Christian beliefs. I don't think it's practicable to imagine that by totally disarming you would prevent them from attacking you. It's a very sad fact, but one has to take note of what has happened all down the ages and is still happening.

The sanguine approach that Richards took to his work was very similar to most of his fellow officers. However, he had his own methods of dealing with the considerable stresses involved in the job.

I used to sing to myself a hymn when I was dealing with a difficult fuze all alone at the bottom of a shaft. It starts:

> *In heavenly love abiding*
> *No change my heart shall fear*
> *For safe is such confiding*
> *And nothing changes here.*
> *The storm may roar about me*
> *My heart may low be laid*
> *But God is round about me*
> *How can I be dismayed?*

I believe there is a whole dimension of real existence, which we only very partially understand and can't expect to fully understand. If we believe in a god who created us and created the universe, as little creatures we ought not to expect to understand more than a tiny fraction. But I think there is an enormous body of evidence to show that there is a dimension to existence, which is just as real as love, which you can't see or measure, but is equally important. The communication between people and what we call for convenience God is a reality and one that we should recognize.

For Bryan Richards, being at the bottom of a shaft with a bomb took on a spiritual significance that would never leave him: 'It was just a feeling, a feeling of not being alone although, physically, obviously I was. It is quite an invaluable experience for anyone: to be able to recall a time when they felt a presence with them not of this world is something to treasure.'

5

The mine menace at sea

Suddenly there was a loud up-thrust and a loud bang. My body went absolutely stiff and my head sort of crunched. Then everything went deadly still. It seemed like an hour, but it was possibly only two seconds. The whole ship bounced up and down.

JOHN HARRISON, FORMER CREW MEMBER HMS *BELFAST*

BY ITS NATURE a mine is not something that has 'failed' to explode: a waiting mine is 'yet to explode'. However, mines share with bombs the same goal: to explode and destroy. They bring with them a similar set of problems to those faced by Army bomb disposal men. A book dealing with the problems of explosive ordnance during the Second World War cannot ignore – indeed, must celebrate – the Royal Navy's involvement. In particular, it is the contribution of Lieutenant Commander John Ouvry and Lieutenant Roger Lewis, harking back to the early months of the war, which can be marked out as crucial. Luck threw them a puzzle which, through their skill and bravery, they solved. If it were not for the actions of these two naval officers in November 1939, the war may very well have been over by Christmas that year.

While having the same essential function, bombs and mines are strategically deployed in very different ways. A bomb is designed to explode either on impact or at a predetermined time after arming. The armourer has total control. A mine is a different kind of weapon: it is designed to wait – and wait and wait. It waits until the object it is designed to destroy causes it to explode. In essence the target is 'in control'. For example, a child runs on to a piece of uncleared ground, and its weight is enough to cause the mine to detonate. But there are means of activating mines other than pressure. Some mines are sensitive to movement, light or, in the case of the most troublesome of mines in the Second World War, by the magnetic polarity or the sound of a ship passing nearby. These were known as influence mines.

Hitler alluded to these in a speech he made on 19 September 1939 in Danzig. The might of Germany's war machine was plain for the world to see and he thought it entirely possible that France and Britain would sue for peace in light of their own ill-preparedness. To push things along, he talked of 'our possession of a weapon which cannot be used against us but which we will use against Britain and France if they persist in continuing the war'. What was this 'secret weapon'? All kinds of rumours abounded – among them death rays, nerve gas, aerial torpedoes and even anthrax.

The first few months of hostilities became known as the 'phoney war', as life on the home front carried on much the same as normal. Rationing was yet to be introduced, and conscription was not fully in force. The maritime toll, however, was mounting. In one week in November 1939 fifteen merchant ships were sunk. In the months that followed this total would rise to 128 downed ships within sight of the British coast, their cargoes lost along with many of their crew. The estuaries of the Thames, Tyne, Humber, Forth and Severn were almost totally blockaded, and shipping was able to move in only narrow stretches of the Channel. The years that Germany had spent arming itself had paid off. Out of twenty-two German destroyers in operation, seventeen were being used to lay Hitler's secret weapon.

The nature of the weapon appeared to be revealed through Captain Patrick Dane, whose ship, the SS *Africa Shell*, had been sunk by the German pocket-battleship *Admiral Graf Spee*. The battleship's mission had been to sink as many Allied ships in the Atlantic as possible, and by the late autumn of 1939 her total included nine British merchant ships. Fortunately for those on board the SS *Africa Shell*, the captain of the *Admiral Graf Spee* would rescue defeated enemy crews before sinking the ship. It was in this way that Captain Dane found himself in conversation with Captain Hans Langsdorff of the German Navy, and being told that Nazi chiefs considered the magnetic mine crucial to their winning the war.

The *Admiral Graf Spee* was sunk in the Battle of the River Plate that autumn and Captain Dane was released into Allied hands. The details of his debriefing confirmed what had become the Royal Navy's worst fears. They had no means of dealing with influence mines and, without a specimen to examine, they were never going to get close to finding a solution.

German destroyers were entering British waters at night and laying mines as close to land as possible, sometimes as close as 10 kilometres from shore. U-boats (German submarines) joined in laying a small number of influence mines on the seabed and, untethered, these mines were causing chaos. The British government was indignantly self-righteous. In the House of Commons on 21 November Prime Minister Neville Chamberlain was asked by Labour's Clement Attlee what the government proposed to do about mines in British waters. Chamberlain said:

The House will be aware that during the last three days upwards of ten ships, six of which were neutrals, were sunk with very serious loss of life, by German mines. The Hague Convention to which Germany is a party and which she announced her intention of observing as recently as September 17th last, provides that when anchored mines are used every possible precaution must be taken for the security of peaceful navigation. This is the very essence of the Convention, as the mine cannot discriminate between warship and merchant ship, or between belligerent and neutral.

The story was buried on page 8 of *The Times*, under the headline 'Fresh Outrage', but the impact of the loss of so many ships cannot be underestimated. Sea cargo provided the vast majority of imports to Britain, which at this time was a net importer of food. The country did not produce enough to feed its own population, and relied on imports, especially of grain. If ships from neutral countries refused to enter British waters, Britain could find itself in serious difficulty very quickly.

What was not released to the public was that among the 250,000 tonnes lost in the first three months of the war, there were two of Britain's key warships. The destroyer *Gypsy* was sunk with the loss of thirty lives off Harwich, and HMS *Belfast*, a newly commissioned battle cruiser, had been severely damaged by what was thought to be an influence mine in the Firth of Forth. Despite being one of the most powerful battle cruisers ever built, the damage she sustained was to keep her out of the fleet for nearly three years. The Admiralty admitted the loss of the *Gypsy* but the crippling of the *Belfast* was kept from the public. Unsurprisingly, Chamberlain's tone was far from conciliatory. His speech continued:

> *This fresh outrage is only the culmination of a series of violations of agreements to which Germany had set her hand. I need only recall the sinking of the* Athenia *with the loss of 112 British lives... These attacks have been made often without warning and to an increasing extent, with a complete disregard of the rules laid down in the Submarine Protocol to which Germany subscribed, or of the most elementary dictates of humanity. His Majesty's Government are not prepared to allow these methods of conducting warfare to continue without retaliation.*

Chamberlain's response was to invoke powers to seize any and all goods on board ships regardless of the flag they were flying. This was to prove unpopular with Britain's allies. What is more, starvation in Britain was indeed becoming a serious threat, and in October 1939, in anticipation of the crisis that appeared to be impending, Admiral Raeder of the German Navy predicted in a report to Hitler that Britain would be on its knees within weeks.

Nicho Poland, who reached the rank of Rear Admiral by the end of his career, was then a young lieutenant based at HMS *Vernon*, the Royal Navy's Mine Warfare establishment at Portsmouth. He remembers this period well.

Between September '39 and March '40, 128 vessels were sunk on the east coast. I remember coming down in June of '40 and seeing the masts sticking up along the Barrow Deep. If we hadn't been able to take effective steps then I think we would have gone under. It only takes a month for this country to be starved out in war. Of course the media was telling people that it was a phoney war. But from a naval point of view it was far from a phoney war. The Germans had twenty-two destroyers and three-quarters of those were running up and down the east coast laying ordinary moored mines. Suddenly we found ourselves in November '39 facing the fact that mines up and down the east coast sank about a hundred ships, and we hadn't the faintest idea how to deal with it.

Those who were on board HMS *Belfast* at the time recall that there was something 'different' about this kind of mine. John Harrison was below decks when the explosion occurred:

When I got out on deck we were told that our keel was hanging off. Now to blow this [ship] so high that a destroyer escort could tell us our keel was hanging off... It has an 18-foot draft so it must have been lifted up at least 20-odd feet out of the water to see the bits hanging off our keel. Ridiculous! We're talking about a 10,000-tonne-displacement ship. That shows the power of a magnetic mine. No wonder I had a headache the next day.

The *Belfast* survived because it was one of the first ships to be welded and not riveted. The added strength allowed it to eventually be brought back into service – not an option for the fleet of both military and merchant ships required to keep Britain alive. Without a specimen for the research scientists to take apart, it was impossible to know how to deal with this threat. But within twenty-four hours of Chamberlain's speech the tide would literally turn and Britain would be on the way to winning the war. Hitler's 'secret weapon' would be secret no more.

The true scale of the impending disaster was indeed being kept from the public at large and it would seem that there were many politicians who preferred not to acknowledge the perilous state that Britain was in. *The Times* on 24 November ran a timely article written by the newspaper's naval correspondent with the headline 'German Device No Novelty'. It expressed concern that the term 'magnetic mine' was causing confusion:

Many people appear to have pictured the magnetic mine as floating freely in the sea, being as it were sucked into contact with any steel ship passing near it by magnetic attraction and exploding on contact... No such mine could exist outside the imagination of the pseudo scientist devoid of all practical knowledge of magnetism.

The expression appears to have originated with the captain of the Danish ship Canada, *who at the official inquiry... into the fate of his ship, gave it as his opinion that she had been sunk by a mine which, by magnetism, exploded on the near approach of his ship without actually coming into contact.*

The *Times* naval correspondent could have had little idea of the drama that was about to unfold as he penned this article, and still less of the barely suppressed panic that filled the corridors of the Admiralty. But the propaganda machine was running at full tilt.

There is no scientific impossibility, or even great difficulty, in fitting such a magnetic device to a mine; nor is there any great novelty. The Admiralty is well aware both of the possibility of such devices and of the methods of dealing with them.

Just as in 1914–18 it was necessary to devise and provide the methods and organization necessary to protect shipping against the German mines of that day, which were considerably in advance of contemporary British mines – so a similar necessity reappears today. There is, however, this difference. The art of mining, and consequently the counter-art of mine clearance, had been neglected in the British Navy in the years before 1914. But the serious consequences of that neglect were fully realized after the last war; and there should be no such delay as was then experienced in the defence overtaking the attack... In any case, it is clear that the exaggerated forecast of the effect of the new weapon cannot be sustained.

There was, however, one politician who was taking notice. At this stage the First Lord of the Admiralty, Winston Churchill, would not be Prime Minister for another seven months, but in his role as the government's voice within in the Royal Navy his proactive involvement would be crucial. Nicho Poland remembers Churchill's foresight:

Not all politicians understood the seriousness of the situation, but Churchill did. He was then First Lord of the Admiralty, remember, not Prime Minister. He said, 'I want a report every evening on how you are progressing, whether it was mine detection ships or double 'L' sweeps or whatever.' Churchill really did play his part. He realized we were practically on our knees. One hundred and twenty-eight ships in a few months? We couldn't go on like that.

The shore base HMS *Vernon* was responsible for the development of underwater weapons of all kinds, such as torpedoes and mines. It was also supposed to be responsible for research into defences against underwater weapons. Captain Denis Boyd was the key research scientist there at the time. Rear Admiral Poland remembers *Vernon* and Boyd well:

> Vernon *in peacetime was an extremely pleasant place to serve. Going right back to my childhood, I remember going to children's parties there. The even tenure of life was rather interrupted in 1938 by the Munich crisis. Just before that Denis Boyd had been appointed as a captain. He was an extremely far-sighted and courageous officer and he sent a number of signals to the Admiralty and a number of letters urging them to spend money on finding an antidote to influence mines, particularly the magnetic mine. He got a message back saying as this form of sweep was only required in wartime it need not be developed in peacetime. He framed that and stuck it over his desk.*
>
> *The picture I would like to give is of this dynamic captain arriving, seeing what needed to be done and getting the cold shoulder by the Admiralty in peacetime. But when the call came, he was ready.*

And so were his men. Lieutenants John Ouvry and Roger Lewis were to play a major part in enabling Britain to keep its ports open and its shipping fleet moving, and consequently allowing it to stay in the war.

Ouvry, an expert in mines, had been aware of the crisis that was building and for eleven weeks had been waiting to hear that one of these mystery mines had been found. He had been asleep at a hotel in London's Victoria when the call came through, with a message that he should report to the Admiralty, the London headquarters of the Royal Navy. Nicho Poland knew Ouvry and his background well, just as he knew that his speciality had not been seen as a priority in the interwar years.

We neglected the unfashionable parts of the Navy, which were minesweeping, anti-submarine warfare; anything that went on underwater was unprofessional. And yet at the same time at Vernon *we had in the mine department some very fine officers. John Ouvry had been passed over for commander. He never grumbled at all about being passed over; he just loved his job in the mining section. A lot of jobs came his way and he didn't really concentrate on the magnetic mine until the war called upon him to do so.*

Tensions at the Admiralty were high as the true state of affairs was becoming increasingly obvious. The destroyer *Gypsy* was sunk, the Thames and Humber estuaries were heavily mined, as was the channel at Harwich. Officers had been sent to Southend, Harwich and Grimsby to try to determine what was going on, but there was no hard evidence coming back. The skipper of a ship called the *Yarmouth Trader* had marked the location where he had seen one drop into seven fathoms of water. The Admiralty even offered £1,000 to any diver willing to go down and look at it.

Influence mines were suspected but, contrary to the confidence with which *The Times* was viewing the 'crisis', without proof everyone just had to sit on their hands and wait. In Ouvry's own understated words, 'The situation was becoming acute.' But then, just as things were looking hopeless, a breakthrough came. Increased levels of vigilance around the coasts had paid off. Between nine and ten o'clock on the evening of 22 November a German aircraft was seen dropping an object that looked like a soldier's kit bag attached to a parachute into the water off Shoeburyness in Kent. The waters in this area were shallow and it was realized that at low tide, the object that was assumed to be a parachute mine would be exposed to view.

Following his wake-up call, a car was booked to take Ouvry and Roger Lewis, a torpedo man, to Southend, near Shoeburyness, at 1 a.m. Low tide was to be at 4 a.m. and their orders were to recover the parachute mine 'at all costs'. Neither of them could be under any illusion that their own lives could well be included in the final bill, but at least the waiting was over.

Ouvry's experience had long been telling him that the most likely kind of mine they would be dealing with was an influence mine. Most mines worked on contact: when they hit a ship, they exploded. Influence mines could lie undetected on the sea floor and were set off either by the ship passing over them (magnetic) or the regularity of the sound made by the ships propeller (acoustic). There had even been magnetic mines used by the British towards the end of the First World War but the neglect of Britain's own mines development in peacetime had meant that this technology had been largely forgotten. At least *The Times* had been right about that part of the story.

Ouvry and Lewis arrived off Southend to see huge numbers of ships still in the Channel, unable to move in any direction until the mines were cleared. The care that was needed was highlighted when a ship carrying frozen meat swung round in the tide and set off a mine. Taking apart a mine that was sensitive to this degree was not going to be easy. A party of soldiers with lights, ropes and a photographer was awaiting them in the pouring rain. Ouvry's report, written shortly after the operation was over, describes his first encounter with the mine:

A private led the cavalcade, splashing through the pools of water left by the receding tide, until the light of our torches showed us a dark menacing-looking object lying partially embedded in the sand. Lewis and I then advanced to the attack, the soldiers in the rear illuminating the mine by Aldis lamp. It was cylindrical in shape, made of some aluminium alloy, had tubular horns on the nose and a hollow tail containing a massive phosphor bronze spring. There were two unpleasant looking fittings near the fore end and these looked like being our Public Enemies Nos. 1 and 2.

The first of these enemies was a valve with which Ouvry was familiar, but the second was something he had never seen before. It was a device made of polished aluminium and secured to the mine by means of a screwed-on ring made watertight with tallow. There also seemed to be some kind of safety device: a 'tear off' strip was still attached. Ouvry guessed that this device would harbour the primer and detonator. It had to be tackled first. However, there was a major problem. At this point Ouvry had no idea whether the mine was acoustic or magnetic. It could even be neither. Nevertheless, it was essential that any tools he used were made of a non-magnetic material. They had already removed all their metal buttons, buckles, coins and cigarette cases. No chances were going to be taken. Normal spanners, screwdrivers or hammers could result in him and Lewis being blown to bits.

Poland remembers hearing about the way this problem was overcome. Ouvry made an impression of the fitting on a pad of paper by pressing it down around the device. It needed a four-pin spanner. There was nothing in their non-magnetic tool kit that was even close.

They had to get non-magnetic tools made at the local Shoeburyness gun range. It was a gunnery officer who came to the rescue and made these special tools to fit the various hexagonal nuts and bolts in the mines. It became a joint thing – gunnery and torpedo. Normally we were not exactly daggers drawn, but friendly rivals!

It was still the middle of a filthy wet night and the waters were rising as the tide turned. Ouvry and Lewis dared not do anything to the mine until the correct tools were available and so the soldiers lashed down the mine and they headed off to await daylight. The mine would be visible again by 12.30 p.m. As they made their way to the shore they saw a light in the distance. Their suspicions were aroused and they moved towards it. It vanished as they approached it. Tensions were still very high and all were aware that the winning of the war could depend on the next few hours.

Just after dawn a message arrived that another mine had been spotted about 300 metres from the one they had been looking at. The tide was coming in rapidly and by the time they reached the area, the water was too deep. There was nothing they could do but wait for the tide to recede. By 1 p.m. they were able to proceed. It was decided that Lewis should remain on the shore as Ouvry and Chief Petty Officer Baldwin would tackle the first mine. In the event of anything going wrong, at least Lewis would have observed it and, in dealing with the second, could hopefully avoid the same mistake. A tractor lorry with a crane attached stood by optimistically waiting to collect a precious cargo.

Ouvry went to work. At 1.37 p.m. Baldwin handed Ouvry the newly machined spanner, aware that it was more than likely that a German booby-trap lay in wait, ready to activate as the first screw was loosened. The spanner fitted and slowly Ouvry unscrewed the ring a fraction of a turn. Gently he continued to turn it. It loosened with remarkable ease and both men were still alive. So far, so good. After a few more turns the ring was free; Ouvry took a small brass rod and prised it into the opening. What he saw was either a detonator or some kind of magnetic needle device. He lowered the rod into the hole and fished around until he hooked the fitting, pulling it out very slowly, all the time aware that the detonator would contain enough explosive to kill both him and Baldwin. Ouvry removed it entirely and he, Baldwin and Lewis (who was watching through binoculars) breathed a sigh of relief.

Twenty-two long minutes had passed and Ouvry looked back down into the hole. There appeared to be a tubular disc of some kind of explosive together with a primer. No amount of poking around could free them, but, believing that he had removed the most dangerous part, he sent Baldwin ashore to fetch Lewis. They needed to manhandle the mine so that the primer could be removed and the fitting that was still buried in the sand could be reached. Together they tied a rope around the mine and rolled it over so that the loose primer discs could be extracted. Then they had to use brute force to detach two plates, the second of which concealed the detonator carrier. It was electric and to their surprise and great relief they recognized it. It was the same as the one used in the German horned mine. 'We felt on top of the world!' reported Ouvry.

The remaining parts of the mine were removed, including the last extraction of a cylindrical object with a valve at one end and five leads connecting it through a hole in the casing to an invisible object within the mine. It was the arming clock. Then the mine was hoisted on to the lorry and sent ashore to be stored. The whole operation had taken just under two hours and Ouvry's hands had been steady throughout. Poland recalls his reactions:

He was nervous but he was so intent on studying the job that his hand kept steady. He told me that his hands never shook at all. There was no time to be frightened and if his hand shook it was disturbing the magnetic balance of the mine and he might have gone up with it. He was such a marvellous chap. He never talked about it; you had to ask him. He was a true hero, as was Roger Lewis.

Lewis laid down the arming clock and it started to tick. They all made a run for it, aware that any device could harbour a booby-trap. There was relieved laughter all round when it was found to be the clock movement starting in the casing, and, as such, no danger. There was not much time to relax, however, as Lewis was told to report to the Admiralty that evening. It was 11.15 p.m. by the time he arrived and he was astonished to see nearly a hundred people assembled in the largest room in the building. He was seated between the First Lord of the Admiralty, Sir Winston Churchill, and Admiral Sir Dudley Pound, as he recounted the efforts of John Ouvry and the team at Shoeburyness. Churchill was aware of what was at stake but at the time even he was unaware of the debt owed to the actions of these men. At the end of the meeting, Churchill promised to call *Vernon* immediately to tell them that work must proceed 'day and night' to find out exactly what they were dealing with at this point. It was only once the mine was examined in detail that serious countermeasures could be put into place.

Meanwhile, Ouvry had left Southend to go to the Woolwich Arsenal where so much research into explosive devices was being done. He took with him the mysterious aluminium fitting he had removed first from the mine. An X-ray failed to reveal its innards adequately but they did suspect that it was a type of time delay fuze. Subsequent examination proved this to be correct. Ouvry then carried on back to *Vernon* where the mine was soon to follow on the evening of 24 November. Poland remembers that they were still unsure as to exactly what kind of mine this was. He also remembers a kind of admiration:

> Like most things German, it was well engineered but it wasn't more than we would have expected. As a matter of fact we didn't really know whether it was going to be an acoustic mine or a magnetic mine. To start with, when Roger Lewis went up to see Churchill at the Admiralty he first of all said it would be an acoustic mine.

Churchill's message that work was to continue without delay was adhered to and within twelve hours they knew all there was to know. The mine was indeed magnetic. By finding the answer, an even bigger question was posed. How was it to be counteracted?

Almost immediately all sorts of weird and wonderful solutions for sweeping were put forward: magnets were attached to flat fish, live goats were used, bar magnets were towed behind ships. But another immediately pressing problem was whether there was any way in which ships could be made immune to setting off the mine. The mine was detonated by the ship's own polarity: steel ships have an innate polarity and, like every piece of ferrous metal, a magnet is attracted to it. If the ship could be demagnetized in some way, then the mine would fail to detonate. The solution was cumbersome but effective. Electric cable was used to girdle all the ships in the British fleet, both merchant and naval. This technique was known as 'degaussing' and proved to be highly effective.

Hitler meanwhile was unaware of the breakthrough against his much vaunted 'secret weapon' and on 29 November issued a directive that the Kriegsmarine (Navy) and Luftwaffe should continue with 'attacks on the principal English ports by mining and blocking sea lanes'. Defeat of Britain was vital to his war aims, and the 'most effective means of ensuring this is to cripple the English economy by attacking it at decisive points'. He knew that 95 per cent of foreign trade went through only a handful of British ports, including London, Liverpool and Newcastle. However, internal political wrangling had swayed him and it was flawed strategy that was to cost Germany the mine-laying battle, as Poland points out:

We were saved by the enmity between Goering and Admiral Raeder. I think Goering wanted to wait until they had more mines and then do a huge, single Luftwaffe operation to close the ports. But Raeder said no, they are in disarray now: let's use our 1,500 magnetic mines at this moment. [The British] are practically on their knees anyhow. But the Luftwaffe wouldn't provide the aircraft to lay the mines. They had a few old planes and very badly trained crews. They made an awful mess of it and dropped two on the mud at Shoeburyness. That saved the day...

The collision of a number of factors had come to Britain's rescue: the Germans should have waited until they had enough of their new mines to implement them properly. Had they done so, shipping would have been even more badly hit than it already was. The Luftwaffe pilots, who were for this mission under Navy control, should have been better trained. Dropping their cargo of mines over tidal estuaries was not particularly clever and was bound to lead to the recovery of at least one sooner or later. Lastly, the combined efforts of John Ouvry, Roger Lewis and the cross-service team at Shoeburyness – together with not a little luck – was the essential ingredient that led Britain to a way through this crisis. In his memoirs entitled *The Gathering Storm*, Churchill noted that although the anxiety surrounding the mine problem continued to a degree, from this point on the 'menace' was controlled. The threat began to recede as methods to counteract the mine were developed, and by Christmas 1939 Churchill was able to write to the Prime Minister of 'marked success'.

The support of Churchill ensured that mine warfare was duly given the resources it needed and Poland remembers how the renewed vigour with which research was undertaken helped: 'The mine department at HMS *Vernon* was developed very rapidly and "tit for tat" went on throughout the war. We were always in the lead, mainly because of the wonderful spirit of *Vernon* and its research establishment.'

However, HMS *Vernon* did not escape tragedy. As the research work continued and countermeasures developed, it was not very long before Germany raised the stakes by introducing a counter countermeasure of their own to deter any investigation. On 5 August 1940 a mine had been recovered from a field in Kent. It was made safe in the field and, as was the norm, was sent on to *Vernon* for further investigation. The team there began to take the mine apart and by the next morning the operation was well advanced. The officer who had brought the mine in, Lieutenant C. A. Hodges, visited the shed and was pleased to see that the dismantling was proceeding apace. As he left the shed to cross the harbour, a huge explosion rang out and he turned to see the building disintegrate before his eyes. The commander in charge of the mining department arrived to find chaos: the roof was no more and bloody body parts lay scattered around. In all, six men died.

Later debriefings revealed what appeared to be a new type of booby-trap. Lieutenant J. Glenny, who had successfully defuzed the second mine at Shoeburyness and was by now very experienced, had been observing Chief Petty Officer Fletcher remove the rear door of the mine. A strange 'whirring' noise was heard, a flash of light, then an enormous explosion. When the mine was put back together it was found that there was an electrically fired charge, the circuit for which was completed when a stud in the rear door was removed. The damage was caused by only one kilo of explosive, a small fraction of what the mine contained. Mysteriously, the charge was not designed to activate the total explosive power of the mine. Had it done so, there would have been precious little of *Vernon* left and many, many more casualties. The booby-trap's sole purpose was to kill the team who were stripping it.

Over the next days and weeks, work courageously continued in the face of this deterrent. Germany had not reckoned on the bravery of the men of HMS *Vernon*. A solution was soon found but not before a new problem had emerged; mines were deliberately being dropped on built-up areas. The Royal Navy's involvement in 'bomb' disposal was not limited to mines that fell in the sea. The Germans had realized that their mine technology had a place on land too. They had developed a fuze that would activate if the mine were to fall into water less than 13 feet (4 metres) deep, essentially to prevent recovery and analysis of its workings. When it was released from an aircraft, a clockwork mechanism started which armed the fuze. When the mine landed, on either water or land, another clock would start to run for seventeen seconds. This was designed to allow the mine to sink to a depth at which the water pressure would force a rubber seal to close, so stopping the clock and leaving the mine armed to await a passing ship. If the water pressure were not there, the clock would run out its seventeen seconds and detonate the mine.

On the night of 16/17 September 1940 an estimated twenty-five mines were dropped on London of which some seventeen failed to explode. Of the ones that did explode the blast damage was immense. Unlike bombs, which were designed to penetrate buildings before exploding, mines – having virtually floated down on their parachutes – would frequently explode at roof level. With nothing to absorb the blast, the devastation covered several hundred square metres. This was reflected by the size of the evacuation area required for each unexploded mine: 385,000 square metres, roughly the equivalent of ninety football pitches. Colonel Stuart Archer recalls the impact made by the mines, and the possible reason for the German tactics:

It so happened that because they were on parachutes they were dropped badly. I think it was on Clacton that two or three of these parachute mines were dropped and, of course, they went off. They did vast damage because of their high explosive content – 10 feet long, 2 feet in diameter, all explosive except a thin aluminium case round the outside. They ripped literally hundreds and thousands of roofs.

He remembers that a news report had slipped through the censors' net, giving details of the devastation: 'This gave Jerry the idea, "Oh good, we won't drop the bloody things in the estuaries any longer, we'll drop them over the towns."'

The responsibility for the disposal of mines, regardless of where they fell, lay with the Royal Navy. A team was hastily assembled. It drew in any officer at HMS *Vernon*, the torpedo school at Chatham and the Admiralty who had some experience of this type of mine. In total the team numbered only nineteen officers and was supported by an extremely courageous group of junior officers and ratings. Meanwhile, Army bomb disposal teams who were in the area were warned by the War Office as to the extreme sensitivity of the mines and that they were not to be approached without the guidance of a member of the Navy team. Not only would any ferrous object such as belt buttons, buckles or tools set off the mines, they were also sensitive to the slightest vibration. Even a passing truck or train could cause a mine to explode once armed.

An immunizing method for the magnetic mine had been developed at *Vernon* which involved tricking the fuzing mechanism into thinking it was at pressure, and either preventing the clock from starting or, if it had already started, halting its progress. It was known as the Safety Horn and with the Heath Robinsonesque panache that was to come to characterize most immunizing machinery, its principal components consisted of brass tubing and the rubber bulb from a motor horn. A bicycle pump was used via a tap to pressurize the bulb, which when transferred to the fuze head created enough pressure to convince the fuze that it was in water deeper than 4 metres. Once this was done, it was possible to remove the locking ring and detach the fuze.

In yet another twist to the 'cat and mouse' game that had come to characterize work in bomb disposal, German intelligence had led to a simple alteration being made to foil British efforts. But despite these frequent changes, the work had to continue – albeit with ever-heightened vigilance.

There were barely enough men to deal with the number of mines that were dropping. Very quickly the Admiralty realized that nineteen officers could not be expected to carry on without support for what was now looking like a long war. They were also among the most skilled in their field and were desperately needed back in their posts for further research work. By 26 September 1940 a new grouping was formed, drawn largely from the volunteers of the Royal Naval Reserves of both Britain and Commonwealth countries. To add further to the pressures of the situation, supplies of the immunizing devices were desperately short and for most teams their 'specialist' equipment amounted to a length of string with which to pull out the fuze from a moderate distance. This length of string added only slightly to the safety margin of seventeen seconds' warning given if the officer was lucky enough to hear the clock start. If truth were told, it was unlikely he could get far enough away to survive; many men were to die in the sprint from almost inevitable death.

But there were several tales of luck mixed with liberal doses of heroism, among them two volunteer officers called Lieutenant R. S. Armitage and Sub Lieutenant H. E. Wadsley. They managed to cover thirty yards when they heard the clock start to tick. Both were thrown through the air, badly shaken and bruised, yet amazingly they still turned up for duty the next day.

Because of this seventeen-second warning, 'funk-holes' became common. This involved finding or creating a place to run to that would offer some protection if the clock started ticking. Measuring out the distance in which one could run in seventeen seconds became part of the routine of mine defuzing and, as one officer said, it was better that the hole they dug or wall they used be fractionally too close than just out of reach.

By early October 1940, 183 mines had been dealt with in London; of these, nine had exploded while being made safe. But the onslaught was far from over and the mines being found were not all magnetic. Different types of mines were dropped and given letter codes. The 'C' mine was magnetic but by 1941 a new variant was being used – the 'G' mine, which incorporated an anti-stripping device. Major Lionel Meynell of the Royal Engineers, who as we saw in Chapter 2 had been severely injured the previous year in a bomb explosion, recalls an unwelcome encounter with one of these new varieties:

> We got a report of a new type of mine called the 'G' Mine. It could be identified by its tail fins, which were blue bakelite. I was based in Coventry and we had the most terrific raid on Nuneaton. I went up there and we found some of these blue tail fins. We were compelled to notify the Navy about this and they came along. They said, it's magnetic, it's acoustic and it's got a photo-electric cell as well as one or two other things.

The Navy explained the restrictions these devices would mean to the way the men could work.

> They said to us there must be no magnetic material used at all: you have to use bronze spades, no studs in your boots; you mustn't completely uncover the mine because the photo-electric cell will work. We'll need to come back at night to uncover it and paint it over with black paint to prevent the light getting in and setting it off. As well as that, the pattern of digging must be controlled. You don't just dig, dig, dig, dig, dig – you dig, dig, dig, pause, dig, dig, pause – vary the pattern of digging. The acoustic part was timed to go off in response to a ship's propeller. It was a constant sound that would detonate the

mine, so the pattern of noise had to be varied. The Navy went on to deal with the rest of it. They would get into it, cut the wires and the bits and pieces. Our responsibility – finished.

Mines continued to be dropped throughout the war, targeting all the major industrial cities as well as port areas. The port of Liverpool was key to Britain's war effort, and it was here that one of the most remarkable tales of the Second World War was to be set, with Lieutenant Commander H. R. Newgass as its main character.

Harold Newgass was born in 1899 and volunteered as a sub lieutenant in the reserves at the age of forty-one – considerably older than most of his colleagues. He was sent to the Garston Gas Works in Liverpool. A mine had fallen through a gasometer and had caused 6,000 people to be evacuated and the railway lines to the docks to be closed, while posing a serious threat to the supply of gas to a large part of the city. As it fell, the mine had burst through the gasometer roof and was suspended by its parachute, which had snagged on the jagged edge of the entry hole. Gas had leaked out, causing the gasometer to fall and so lowering with it the mine, which had come to rest, submerged in the 2 metres (6.5 feet) of stinking, oily water that lay in its base.

Over 5.5 million litres (about a million gallons) of water had to be pumped out before Newgass could even think about making the mine safe. The pumping took several hours and left a thick sticky coating of tar-like sludge on the floor. As if this was not enough, the air remained positively noxious and also highly inflammable. It was into this vision of Hades that Newgass went – alone. The psychological comfort of a 'funk-hole' was not a possibility. There would be no way out should the mine start to tick.

The breathing apparatus available was very basic and allowed Newgass only thirty minutes at a time to work on the mine. By the time he waded in towards it, he had precious few minutes in the murky darkness to work on the fuze. On one trip he took in a ladder and his tools, on the next he undertook the treacherous task of turning the mine round, knowing that the slightest untoward bump could start the clock. It was to take six journeys before his work was complete and with each trip the risk of the mine exploding became greater and greater. Eventually, after several hours' work, the mine was made safe.

For his immense courage in defuzing what was, eerily, Newgass's thirteenth mine, he was awarded the George Cross. Full recognition for his bravery went unrecognized until after the war was over, the lesson of the Clacton mine having now being learnt. However, he could receive the gold cigarette case and cufflinks presented to him by the workers at Garston, plus the numerous gifts from the 6,000 grateful people who returned safely to their homes. Harold Newgass died aged eighty-five in 1984, and his George Cross can now be seen in the Imperial War Museum in London.

Naval Bomb Safety Officers, as they came to be known, worked under the Director of the Unexploded Bomb Department within the Admiralty and, unlike the Royal Engineers, usually worked alone or at the most with two ratings to support them. Of course, there were occasions when more men were needed. Mines were not always above ground. From time to time the parachute on which the mine was supposed to float to earth would fail, causing the mine to descend at a much faster rate than intended. This added velocity meant that the mine would penetrate the ground to a considerable depth. At times like this the digging skills of the Royal Engineers were brought in.

Cecil Brinton, who as we saw in Chapter 3 often took on the duties of an officer, was at this time a sergeant in section 61 of 2 Company Bomb Disposal. He remembers the complicated job involved in trying to remove a mine using only the normal picks and shovels – there being no non-magnetic tools available. They did, however, make good use of the sheer legs (the three metal legs positioned over the bomb shaft and on which a pulley could be mounted).

The most dangerous job I had when I was in bomb disposal was getting out a magnetic mine. They were great big things. There were several types of mines and this one was about nine foot long and three foot in diameter. Most of them were intended to go down into estuaries like the Thames or something like that. Some would miss of course, with the parachutes, but they would come down fairly slowly, and if they came down in an open space they would just go over on their side. But this one in particular, the parachute must have failed to open or it was damaged or something, and it came straight down at speed, like a bomb would and right down into the ground, the full length of it – nine feet!

There was a Naval Officer there some time before us. We went there to provide a workforce to get this thing out. He got us together and he said this is about one of the most dangerous jobs you'll ever have because the fuze is magnetic. If you're digging a pit to get it up with your metal picks and shovels and you get anywhere near that fuze, it could set it off.

The mine was right beside a railway and it had to be taken out because it was a mainline and no traffic could travel. He discovered there was a railway depot just a little way up the line, so he said I think what we'll do is try to pull it out to save you digging. So, we fixed our sheer legs and he went up to the railway depot. They supplied an engine and a big steel rope. We fixed the rope to the mine where the parachute had been attached, tacked it up on our sheer legs, across to the engine which was several hundred yards back. We realised there would be a lot of pressure on this so we put planks under the sheer legs and did our signal to the driver to pull. He started up and the sheer legs went right through the planks! So, we had a rethink.

The next idea was to put metal plates under the sheer legs. The rope was reattached, the engine pulled back but yet again, their ingenuity was in vain:

It showed the pressure and the suction I suppose. It was in clay and as the mine goes through clay it compacts and there must have been so much pressure it snapped the steel rope. The Naval Officer said, 'Well, chaps, I am afraid you are going to have to dig for it.' So we took away the sheer legs and left the rope there with the engine and we started to dig on the side facing the embankment. We would dig down to about two or three inches of it and then get a bit of wood and scrape the remainder away in case the fuze was there. Eventually we got right down to the nose of it – that's nine feet down – and we sloped a trench up towards the embankment. We attached the rope directly on to the mine, went back and signalled... the mine just fell over. It looked so simple; it just went over and slid up the trough on to the ground at the top. Fortunately the fuze had been at the other side. You never know what might have happened if it had been on our side. It only needs a bit of steel of any sort, you know, even our cap badge or something like that. Anything metal could have set it off. But at the time we just had to get on with the job. I had taken so many chances I suppose I was getting immune to it. I thought I had a guardian angel looking after me...

Royal Engineers had worked with Naval officers in a fine example of the kind of cross-service co-operation that was common when dealing with mines. Cecil Brinton had survived this hazardous mission: it was not long before he was to need his guardian angel again, although this time it would be in another country, dealing with a different kind of weapon. As we shall see in the next chapter, the skills of the bomb disposal officer were required in many countries throughout the world.

6

Island fortress

BRITAIN'S IMPERIAL HISTORY meant that many territories around the world were drawn into the war, far from the 'mother country' itself. Wherever there were bombs or mines, the personnel required to dispose of them would follow. Teams from the Army and Navy were sent to such diverse places as Hong Kong, Singapore, Ceylon (Sri Lanka) and North Africa. But never were they needed more than on the island of Malta, which was to face an intense air bombardment unparalleled anywhere during the Second World War. During one month in 1942, more bombs fell on this small, rocky island than on the whole of London during the heaviest months of the Blitz.

Lying at the centre of the Mediterranean, 58 miles (92 kilometres) from Sicily, Malta has always been of great strategic importance. It was colonized in turn by many a conquering empire, from Phoenicians, Greeks and Romans to Arabs and French, before being annexed by Britain in 1814. It then became an important naval base, never more vital than during the Second World War. It was within easy range of North Africa, where from July 1942 the Battle of El Alamein would mark a breakthrough for the Allies and a turning point in the war. Hundreds of British aircraft were stationed on the island, while the harbour at the capital, Valletta, was a key port for ships making the treacherous journey through waters threatened by

German U-boats and warships. However, it was not until Italy joined the war that a major attack on Malta became inevitable. The raids started on 11 June 1940, only seven hours after Italy had declared war on Britain.

At this point the Italian air force's principal targets were the airfields, the port at Valletta and the island's main area of population, the Three Cities area of Senglea, Vittoriosa and Cospicua. For the first seven months the raids were sporadic but, on an island of less than 400 square kilometres (about 150 square miles), the collateral damage was considerable. By December 1940, the Luftwaffe had taken up a position in Sicily, and on 16 January 1941 a hundred aircraft unleashed a terrifying storm of bombs on what appeared to be a sitting duck: the disabled Royal Navy aircraft carrier, HMS *Illustrious*. The vessel had lurched into port for repairs after being bombed at sea by the Luftwaffe. Remarkably, thanks to outstanding anti-aircraft attacks from the ground and intervention from the RAF in the air, the ship was not hit while in harbour. However, this day was to be the beginning of the onslaught that would increase from 250 attacks in the first three months of the year to as much as eight attacks per day during the following May.

Naturally, bombing on this scale was always going to lead to a very heavy workload for those charged with dealing with unexploded bombs. In June 1940, when the first of the raids began, the full implications of the UXB problem were still being absorbed back in the UK. Bomb disposal was in its infancy and although the organization on the British mainland began to take shape quickly following the formation of the Inspectorate of Fortifications and Bomb Disposal, of the 15,000 troops stationed on Malta, very few had any experience of dealing with UXBs. Still fewer had any training.

The Royal Army Ordnance Corps did have a presence on the island and two of their officers, Captain R. L. Jephson-Jones and Lieutenant W. M. Eastman, had both received weapons training, but only on British ammunition. They had never seen or been given any information about German or Italian bombs, let alone having any equipment or direct experience. Nevertheless, they undertook the essential work aided by fifteen volunteer NCOs and sappers from 24 Fortress Company, Royal Engineers, who were on the island in their more traditional role of maintaining and building fortifications and gun emplacements. It was a walk into the unknown for all.

Once a bomb was located, the sappers would be sent back to a safe point while Eastman or Jephson-Jones would start to defuze the bomb. The gathering of information was vital, but staying alive to pass it on was considerably more important. There was no means of communicating between the safe point and the officer who remained with the bomb and it was only when they knew that each action they had performed was safe that they would recall their men and recount how they had achieved it. With so few men available, it was important that all the information they could gather be passed on before it was too late.

In the early months of bombing, with no equipment on the island to help them deal with the bombs, most tools were home-made. That so many men survived this first onslaught was nothing short of miraculous, and their self-acquired knowledge was to prove invaluable to those who followed over the coming years on Malta and in North Africa. By November 1940 this rather ad hoc bomb disposal section was enhanced by the arrival of a fully trained and exceptionally well-qualified bomb disposal officer. Taking the helm, Lieutenant E. E. Talbot had brought with him the latest in immunization equipment from the UK. With both the Italian and German air forces about to attack HMS *Illustrious* and its surroundings only six weeks later, his arrival proved timely.

However, the problems facing bomb disposal sections in Malta were different to those facing their colleagues back in Britain. First, the terrain was very different. Malta is a rocky island with little earth or organic strata. This meant that bombs rarely buried themselves in the ground. Therefore, although no deep shafts needed to be dug they would still be covered in the heavy stone and rock that characterize the island and from which most Maltese buildings are constructed.

Secondly, with the Italian air force also dropping bombs, the types of ordnance that had to be identified were considerably greater in number than those facing bomb disposal sections in the UK. A huge variety of bombs were used against Malta, including small SD2s (which would later feature in a horrific raid against Grimsby on the east coast of England in 1943 – see Chapter 8), rocket-assisted bombs, 1,000-kilogram armour-piercing bombs designed to penetrate the island's thick-walled grain stores, and small Italian anti-personnel bombs known because of their slightly tapered shape as 'Thermos' bombs. The variety of bombs faced by a bomb disposal section that never numbered more than thirty-two men was quite remarkable. Even more astounding is the fact that not one of them was killed while disposing of bombs. Sadly, Lieutenant Talbot did lose his life, but on an RAF bombing mission.

Such was the mountain of work to be done that Talbot's place could not be left empty for long. His replacement arrived in the shape of Lieutenant T. W. T. Blackwell who, highly regarded by his men, became renowned for climbing on to the roof of the barracks and plotting the position of bombs as they fell around the island. He was also notable for his very calm demeanour; it was this calmness under pressure that was to give rise to one very poignant story in which Lieutenant Blackwell showed immense courage.

It was late in the evening of 30 July 1940 when reports came in of a stick of very large bombs coming down. One had passed through a house, demolishing it and burying the inhabitants under tonnes of rubble. As was typical in Malta, the bomb had not buried itself in the ground and could still be seen in the midst of the demolished house. Blackwell approached the bomb and discovered two fuze pockets, both containing number 17 fuzes. Worse still, both were ticking. Fear that the Zus40 anti-withdrawal device might be lying in wait under the fuzes meant that pulling them out by hand or from a remote location was impossible. The bomb could explode at any moment; with a good chance that the people buried under the rubble could still be alive, the only solution was to move the bomb.

Without the benefit of any manual or mechanical lifting gear, Blackwell decided to try to drag the bomb with its ticking fuzes free of the debris. A local policeman, Constable J. Baylis, helped clear a path through the rubble and, using a truck and a short length of rope, the two men tried to pull the bomb free. The path was not clear enough and the bomb became jammed against the rocks. There was only one solution. The bomb would have to be guided by hand through the rough path that they had tried to create. Blackwell volunteered to ease the bomb's path while the policeman drove the truck. Both were in grave danger: given the size of the bomb, if it exploded little would be left of truck or men. As if it were a reminder of the treacherousness of the situation, another bomb from the same stick exploded nearby. If this explosion added to the tension of the situation, it did not deter them and their efforts were rewarded. Eventually the bomb was free of the rubble and taken away to a safe location.

Work could now begin to locate survivors under what remained of the house. Tragically, the wait had been too long and nobody was found alive. Nevertheless, the bravery of both men was recognized: Lieutenant Blackwell received the George Medal and Constable Baylis the British Empire Medal, richly deserved for their ingenuity and courage.

The raids on Malta took place at all hours, day and night. One day in April 1942 will be forever remembered for the incredible escape of the congregation attending an early evening service in the island's beautiful Mosta Church. There were three hundred people attending a service as the raid began and, while most ran for shelter in the small chapels that lined the main transept, many remained kneeling amid the deluge from above. Suddenly, a bomb crashed through the church's dome, deflected twice off the walls and travelled the whole length of the church before sliding to a stop. The bomb weighed in at 500-kilograms but mercifully contained only a simple impact fuze that failed to explode. Even so, the damage that occurred was considerable and the fact that nobody was killed was viewed as nothing short of a miracle. The bomb was taken away, steamed out and returned to the church, where it was put on public display as a permanent reminder of what many believed to be a sign of divine intervention.

The RAF had its own bomb disposal team on the island. While the divisions in work were delineated along the same lines as those in the United Kingdom – with the RAF responsible for disposal work on their property, the Royal Navy on ships and port property and the rest falling to the Army – with equipment and manpower in such short supply, cross-service co-operation was essential. Malta's strategic position and importance as a base for offensive operations against German troops in North Africa and beyond meant that its airfields were under increasing pressure, and it became clear that the enemy's objective was not only to destroy aircraft and landing strips, but also to prevent the repair and operation of the airfields. They did this by using a combination of ordnance – bombs with impact fuzes and delayed action bombs, as well as anti-personnel devices that would prevent people from entering the areas to defuze the bombs.

Flight Lieutenant D. Bishop had arrived in Malta early in the war as an armourer with the rank of sergeant. He was quickly promoted and, having been given responsibility for bomb disposal at the Luqa airfield, he was given a day's instruction in the various techniques that were available. As the war progressed, bomb disposal became more than just a sideline for him, and after a move to the Hal Far station he was allocated a small truck in which to carry his stethoscope (borrowed from the sick bay) and accessories including a red flag and whistle, both of which were to become essential to Bishop's way of working. When he entered the airfield to examine the UXB he would ask the control tower to keep an eye on him through their binoculars. If he needed to explode a bomb in situ he would frantically wave the flag at the tower to let them know. They would acknowledge this by firing two rounds from a signal gun. A blast on his whistle would signal detonation was imminent; if successful, he would lay down his flag, prompting the tower to fire another signal to indicate an all-clear. It seemed like a perfect system but not all bombs obliged by falling in open areas, as Bishop was to find out.

At the beginning of May 1942 Bishop was roused from his bed to attend a UXB which had landed next to a naval bomber. He learnt that the bomber was already armed with a torpedo of its own, which, combined with the force from the 500-kilogram German bomb, could make a serious mess of the Hal Far airfield. To complicate matters further, the bomb contained not one but two number 17 fuzes. The logical approach was to move the aircraft away from the bomb. However, when Bishop approached the squadron commander he was informed that while the aircraft could be replaced, the pilot who would have to move it could not.

The bomb casing was split and Bishop examined the possible options, none of which seemed particularly attractive. He decided to try to remove one of the fuze pockets, which appeared on close inspection to be almost free from the bomb. With time desperately short and the fuze ticking away, Bishop started to scoop out the powdered filling around the pocket. He managed to manipulate the pocket sufficiently to get a good grip on the fuze. With the first one free, the danger was only half over and he repeated the operation on the second successfully. The fuzes were quickly deposited in an old bomb crater where they detonated shortly afterwards.

On reporting his exploits to the command armament officer, he was congratulated but reminded of the foolhardiness of his actions. The naval squadron leader had been right to refuse to move the plane: in that instance the pilot was more valuable; similarly, Bishop was told that it was he who was the most valuable man on the island. Without him, they could quickly become paralysed. Nevertheless, a George Medal rewarded Bishop's selfless devotion to duty.

There are hundreds of stories of acts of individual bravery in bomb disposal on Malta: one officer even dealt with a bomb near a hospital while still a patient, while others had to deal with another problem never encountered in Britain – starving and aggressive wildcats that stood guard over one enormous bomb for several hours. Many awards were justly given to the soldiers, sailors and airmen who served on Malta throughout the war but perhaps none was more richly deserved than that given by King George VI at the height of the island's siege. On 15 April 1942 it was the island and its entire population who were the deserved recipients of the highest honour for civilian bravery. The citation read: 'To honour her brave people I award the George Cross to the Island Fortress of Malta to bear witness to a heroism and devotion that will be famous in history.'

7

A change of focus

I can still see people chatting on their doorsteps now. Then, all of a sudden, it was dark.

BACK IN BRITAIN, early 1942 saw a change of pace for bomb disposal. Air raids had become less frequent. There was more time to devote to the backlog of UXBs, while the bomb disposal organization itself was now operating efficiently and responsively. Invasion by Germany looked increasingly unlikely and, with the Allies making progress on foreign fronts, many bomb disposal men were ordered to take up posts abroad. The war in the Far East was still intense and there was work to be done in the Middle East, Gibraltar and Malaya, as well as Malta. Later that year, in November, the Allies had invaded Italy, where the retreating German army had left mines, bombs and booby-traps.

The Royal Engineers who remained in Britain worked on the UXB backlog – there were still substantial numbers of unexploded bombs all over the country. The problem was that many of them were going to require major engineering work to get them uncovered. There was no particular urgency, as it was known that the vast majority of bombs dropped had impact fuzes and as such, if they had not gone off, they were unlikely to do so. Even the dreaded number 17 fuzes, if they had not detonated within seventy-two hours of dropping, were considered safe. Many were in open country, or in places where, even if they did explode, damage to people and property would be negligible.

The Ministry of Home Security had to prioritize resources that were still scarce, and many UXBs were simply left. The Regional Commissioner, whose job it was to categorize bombs, was delegated the task of deciding between the bombs that mattered and those that could wait. (In fact those that were abandoned are still being dug up – at a rate of four or five a year. In May 2000 several thousand people were evacuated from the area surrounding a building site in Bexleyheath while the Royal Engineers defuzed a Second World War bomb, using some of the same techniques employed sixty years ago.)

However, a greater problem was about to make the headlines. On 6 June 1942 there was a massive explosion in the Elephant and Castle area of south-east London. It had been a beautiful day and many of the stoic inhabitants who had lived through the Blitz were out enjoying the warmth of the evening sun. There were two groups of children playing cricket, one at either end of Gurney Street, and the local cinema had just finished its late afternoon showing. As people were strolling home through streets already damaged by bombing, suddenly the ground shook and the sky went black. Danny Slattery was a young boy playing cricket at the far end of the street, fortunately far enough away from the explosion. He recalls: 'Everybody dropped everything. We were playing cricket with an old floorboard and a tennis ball, and all looked up. Bricks were coming down and there were gas pipes, water pipes, all blowing everywhere. We all ran.'

Peter Vigus was walking down a nearby street when he saw an extraordinary sight: 'I looked up and there was a massive cloud of dust. Then I saw a big girder. It must have been about eight or nine foot long. It went right over the top of the first lot of building into Lion Street and hit a roof there. Then, of course, I got up and started running towards where the bomb had gone off. Everyone did that sort of thing – see if you could give a bit of help.'

But not everyone escaped the full force of the explosion. Iris Ward was fourteen years old and had a very close encounter with death. The stress of the experience caused her health to suffer for many years after. The memory is still painful for her.

It was just as if someone had opened a great big oven. The heat rolled, literally rolled up the street. I don't know, but I must have shut my eyes. I felt myself going up and a lamp-post bringing me down. When I opened my eyes everything was dark. I could feel something on top of me. It was either a little girl or a little boy and I thought, 'I can't have this,' and I pushed it off me.

The child who had fallen on top of Iris was one of thirty-seven fatalities that day. Tragically, many were children. The shock of the explosion reverberated across the country, amplified by the unexpectedness of the event. The people of London were almost inured to bombing. Night after night they had trekked to the shelters, never knowing if they would have a home to return to when the all-clear sounded. But for a bomb to explode in daylight when there had not been an air raid for months? The authorities had a serious problem. They had to find a way of reducing the chances of this happening again.

Nobody can be sure whether the devastation on Gurney Street was caused by a large bomb or a mine that had gone unreported. There have been many theories. Some local people speculate that while a bombed house was being demolished, an old water tank had been dislodged and crashed to the ground, setting up a fatal vibration. Others think that the vibration from underground trains running nearby had been enough to set it off. Whatever the reason, action had to be taken

Jimmy Melrose was an officer in 25 Bomb Disposal Company based at Eltham. He remembers being in the mess and hearing that there had been an explosion at the Elephant and Castle.

It really shook the whole of the Civil Defence, the whole of the police, the whole of bomb disposal. It has never been properly explained, but a fairly safe bet was that it was a time delay fuze, which for some reason or another was restarted. But the important thing was that somebody said, 'Wait a minute. We have got to have a good look at this.'

It was now clear that hidden bombs could explode years after they had fallen, and with raids being as intense as they had been, knowing exactly where bombs had fallen was a problem. The authorities had relied on the public reporting where they suspected there was a bomb. To the general public it was extremely difficult to tell whether a small bomb had exploded or a large bomb passing through had caused the damage. Jimmy Melrose explains:

Let's say a smaller bomb had exploded. It would show a considerable evidence of the effects of explosion such as burning, as one would expect. A much larger bomb would probably cause as much as if not more damage to a building on its way down. If there wasn't this evidence of actual explosion then you would say, that's something that must be investigated. Often, people who had been on the site when something had happened came back and said, 'Yes, now that this has been raised there was something that I wasn't terribly happy about.' I mean, I have seen the back of a two-storey house taken right down. You wouldn't blame anyone for saying that it had been a 50-kilogram bomb. In many cases, because it was being done in very heavily blitzed conditions, these things were missed. It's as simple as that.

It was soon realized, however, that it would require more than people with uneasy feelings and hazy memories to come forward. A more structured approach would have to be taken. Every bomb site in the capital would have to be reassessed. Nothing could be taken for granted. Jimmy Melrose was given the job of explaining the signs to look for, and called a meeting at the Odeon Cinema at Elmers End.

This was a meeting we had on a Sunday morning where every-body was invited to come along. I don't think anybody was told they had to be there, but the police, wardens and everyone seemed to turn up. It was a very big meeting. We went over this business and got everyone to rack their memories. Is there anything you've ever had a doubt about?

Melrose went through all the signs, which would differentiate between a bomb that had exploded and one that had just passed through. A bomb that had exploded would typically leave some charring around where it had exploded. He had also taken along some props including a piece of kopfring. Kopfring was a device the Germans had added to their bombs to prevent them penetrating the ground too far. A bomb that exploded at 5 feet (1.5 metres) deep caused much more damage than one that exploded at 30 feet (9 metres). A ring of metal was soldered round the bomb's nose so that when it hit the ground, the ring would help to slow the bomb down. It was attached by some light spot-welds and would usually detach on impact. It was a sure sign that a bomb had fallen. Jimmy Melrose's piece of kopfring was to bring the new initiative's first result.

At the end of this performance, a man came up to me and asked if he could have a look. I showed him [the kopfring]. He said, 'I've had a piece of that holding my shed door open.' I asked him where and it was in West Wycombe. I said, 'I think I'd better come and see this.' I went the following morning and he showed me where this 50-kilogram bomb had exploded right at the back door. We did a little investigation and established that there was a 1,000-kilogram bomb under the back doorstep!

Melrose dispatched a section and the bomb was soon uncovered and defuzed. Over a hundred sites were eventually re-evaluated and twenty-two bombs were discovered as a result. Melrose was on hand to uncover several of them and was aided by one of the latest pieces of technology to be developed: the bomb locator. They were few in number and had been given only to certain sections.

A specialist unit came along on one [excavation] and showed up exactly where they reckoned there was something. When we investigated it we found we were in absolutely virgin sand; it had never been touched since man was on earth. You could tell – the sand was solid and there was no discoloration. I said, 'Supposing this thing is 180 degrees out? Let's go in that direction.' And there, we found a 250-kilogram bomb and the only one in my experience with two 17 fuzes. So that gave us a bit of fun!

The bomb was next to a railway line, and the trains had to keep running. Therefore it had to be defuzed urgently. Jimmy Melrose remembers:

It was the only time in my life that I saw two magnetic clock-stoppers used. They could only just sit on; there was just enough space between the fuzes. These things weighed 180lb each. We were right beside the mainline, which I think had either six or eight tracks so that meant a lot of co-operation was necessary from Southern Railways. I was full of admiration for the way they dealt with things; the way things seemed to get back to normal. I had a site meeting with the superintendent for that particular area. It was a very important set of lines and we agreed that we would let them use the furthest away line. That was no trouble to them; they merely stopped everything and transferred it on to one line, whether it was going into London or out. The condition was that they did not exceed 20 miles an hour.

We could feel it was a sort of place that we were just a wee bit close to the lines. That went fine until one driver either didn't get the message or thought, well, a wee bit faster will do. He went

through and we could feel the whole lot vibrating! So that was the
end of that – we stopped them travelling on those lines altogether.

Jimmy Melrose still remembers with justifiable pride the work that he and his men did: 'It gave a lot of people satisfaction and even now, fifty years later, we still keep hearing that they occasionally find something. If it's in my area I say, "Gee, I missed that!"'

A couple of months before the Elephant and Castle explosion, there had been a change in the Luftwaffe's bombing strategy. Air attacks by now were indeed fewer, but from April they had a definable new focus. Instead of bombing the industrial cities such as London and Birmingham, or the port areas of Plymouth and South Wales, at the behest of Hitler, Goering decided to target Britain's historic cathedral cities. The destruction of greatly loved national treasures might dent the fighting spirit of a people who had yet to show any sign of weakening. The locations for the raids were chosen on the strength of information contained in a series of tourist guides called Baedekers, which still exist today. The cities chosen for what came to be known as the Baedeker raids included Norwich, Canterbury, Exeter, Cambridge and York.

Not expecting such attacks, the cities were not strongly defended – ack-ack guns and barrage balloons were largely confined to the areas which, up until now, had been receiving the heaviest bombing. Now, on the night of 28/29 April 1942, it was York's turn to be bombarded. As it happened, the Minster was undamaged, the bombs landing on the outskirts of the city at a railway marshalling yard. York's marshalling yard was and still is a key point on the east coast main line, and there were upwards of thirty sets of tracks laid side by side. The closure of the station would cause major disruption to the transportation of goods and machinery to the whole country and beyond.

After the raid was over, the unexploded bombs that were found were, unusually, almost all 500 kilograms in weight. These bombs, among the largest in the German armoury, were not normally found in such large numbers; those dotted around the outskirts of the city were dealt with swiftly. However, there was one that posed quite a problem, buried as it was in the middle of a tangle of track at the marshalling yard. Its importance was reflected in its designated category A2 – it had to be dealt with as quickly as possible but detonation in situ was acceptable as a last resort.

Raymond Sharp was an officer based in Leeds when he heard of the raid. He was detailed to deal with the bomb at the marshalling yard: 'We got digging to the bomb as quickly as we could. We had to remove a section of track, which incidentally was quite difficult. Railway lines are pretty heavy and we weren't skilled at the sort of thing.'

It took twenty hours to expose the bomb; they then discovered it contained a 17 fuze and the type 50 anti-handling device. The bomb had only been in the ground for about twelve hours when the digging had started so they were still well within the seventy-two hours for which the 17 fuze could run. Fortunately, it was not ticking. However, the bomb casing was distorted and it was thought that the clockwork mechanism had been damaged, possibly making it rather unstable. The clock-stopper was required as a precaution.

The 17/50 fuze combination was a problem at the best of times. The equipment required to defuse the 17 fuze, the magnetic clock-stopper and battery, were both extremely heavy and unwieldy. In addition, the steam sterilizer was required to steam the TNT out of the bomb casing. This needed a large boiler known as a Merryweather, capable of producing a considerable amount of high-pressure steam to remove the large quantity of explosive. Getting it close enough to the bomb to be useful required some lateral thinking.

In this particular case we couldn't get anywhere near the bomb without transport because on one side was a very high brick wall and the bomb was very close up on that side. In the other direction were about thirty lines of railway. We couldn't get our vehicles over these tracks so we hit on the idea of delivering the apparatus by railway. We got a shunting engine with one truck behind it and we loaded the boiler on with its firing mechanism, and on the front of the shunting engine we put the clock-stopper.

The clock-stopper was attached, the 50 fuze was immunized and two holes were drilled in the bomb casing. Through one the tubing would be inserted for the steam to pass, and from the other the molten TNT could escape. However, the procedure started to go very wrong. The problem stemmed from the very long length of tubing required to run from the boiler to the bomb. The heat was dissipating from the steam before it could reach the TNT. The bomb was also lying in water.

It was rather inefficient in heating and melting the explosive filling. The other thing was that this hole had become very, very wet and we were pumping the water out all the time and, of course, the explosive filling was coming into the water and solidifying. So we were pumping semi-liquid explosive as well as water and the pump began to get clogged up. We were replacing the first length of pipe from the bottom of the hole to the pump about every quarter of an hour and were rapidly running out of hose.

It was decided to explode the bomb in situ. The priority was to get the railway line open again. It was estimated that about a third of the filling was left in the bomb and as much as possible of the semi-solid explosive which was lying around the bomb was removed.

If we had left that material in the bottom of the hole when we fired the bomb, it would have exploded as well as the explosive left in the bomb. We set up an electrically detonated system and blew it up. There was a great big bang, bits of rail all over the place, the station roof was damaged, some of the rolling stock was damaged but within two hours the first goods train ran through.

The explosion had been somewhat bigger than expected but it had the required effect: the trains were running again. On another occasion Raymond Sharp was to have a rather less satisfactory result, when he took a bomb to an old quarry to be disposed of. This particular bomb had been at the company headquarters for some months before Sharp took it to the quarry, ten miles north of Leeds. Quarries were often used for this purpose, and it was a relatively simple procedure to put a charge against the bomb casing, run a detonator wire and explode it. An important part of the operation was to check that the area was clear of people.

It had been steamed out so there was no explosive in it: just the fuze pocket which contained a small amount. We loaded it on to our lorry and went to the quarry, attached the explosive charge and retired to a safe distance behind a screen wall which was used by the quarry people when they used explosives to bring down the stone. Well, there was the most God almighty bang and obviously much greater than just the fuze pocket. It became clear that not all the explosive had been steamed out.

There were houses about 200 metres from the quarry. As Sharp had not expected such a large explosion, he had not thought to evacuate the inhabitants or even warn them.

I thought I'd better just check up on these and see what had happened. I went to the first one and banged on the door. A woman opened it and she was black from head to foot! I went into the house and there was another lady who turned out to be her mother. They looked like chimney sweeps and the whole house was covered with soot that had been forced down the chimneys. I am afraid I thought this was rather funny and I laughed out loud. This woman came at me with a broom and beat me about the head! Quite rightly, too.

Few incidents were to leave an amusing memory for a bomb disposal officer. Raymond Sharp also remembers the time he was detailed to go with another officer and look at a stick of bombs that had fallen in a field in the East Riding of Yorkshire. When they arrived, one of the bombs was unusually exposed, lying close to the surface with its tail sticking out: 'It was quite a small bomb – 50 kilos. So we said to each other that we would get it out ourselves and deal with it. We got a couple of shovels out of the truck and dug down to expose the fuze.'

To their horror it was a 50 fuze in a single fuze pocket. Until this point a single fuze pocket had never been known to contain the anti-handling device. Sharp immediately called back to base and the alert went out.

We immunized the fuze and took the bomb away but there were seven more to deal with, so squads were drafted in from the company. The evening of the next day we had a report that one of the bombs had exploded and we had lost six people – the sergeant in charge and four others. The sixth was a civil defence worker who worked nearby. One chap survived. He was the driver of the truck and he saw what went on. When the bomb was exposed the sergeant had put a rope around it and got his men to pull on it and, of course, it had exploded. Why that happened, goodness only knows. These were experienced people. They knew exactly what to do with this type of fuze and yet they mishandled it and suffered the consequences.

What was the purpose of putting a 50 fuze alone in a bomb? In combination with a 17, it was a very effective means of ensuring that if the bomb was uncovered before the scheduled time of explosion, defuzing it would be very difficult. Putting a fuze that would be activated only by movement implied that it was meant to explode only when someone tried to touch it. Could this be a new strategy? Were the Nazis targeting the bomb disposal officer? Major John Hudson believes that this was not a major strategical development intended to win the war: 'It was just some boffins in the German fuze business who thought it would be a good wheeze. No more than that.' The new year of 1943 was to usher in a new but short-lived era in the fuze war.

Herbert Erich Ruehlemann, the inventor of the electric fuze, and his team at Rheinmetall had developed a new fuze. As John Hudson said, 'It was a trifle in terms of the war effort, but it was a very important trifle as far as bomb disposal officers were concerned: it was deliberately trying to catch them.' Once again, in countering this new threat – the Y fuze, as it came to be known – a mixture of luck, skill and dogged ingenuity prevailed, but not before a few seriously anxious days had passed.

The fuze was found exclusively in 500-kilogram bombs that had fallen and failed to explode during a raid on London on the night of 17/18 January 1943. One of the bombs was deemed to be of the highest priority due to its position near Lord's Cricket Ground, which was being used by the RAF at the time, and its proximity to the Bakerloo line of the London Underground. Captain F. Carlyle was given the duty of disposing of the bomb. Reaching it did not take long and the fuze was identified as a 25B, a direct impact fuze and similar in its operation to the 15. However, in addition to the numerical marking on the fuze head, there was a letter Y. It was not uncommon to see different letters and markings on fuze heads – the Germans' methodical approach ensured that their ammunition could be traced back to source – so at the time, the mark did not seem to have particular meaning. It was the encircled number that was of importance – or so Captain Carlyle thought.

As was usual when dealing with a 25 fuze by this stage in the war, the liquid discharger was used. A discharging fluid was forced into the fuze head at pressure. This was a conducting fluid and would allow the capacitors to discharge without allowing enough energy to be conducted through the fuze to detonate the bomb. It had proved to be a very efficient way of immunizing bombs – until now. Carlyle noticed that only a quarter of the usual amount of fluid had been forced into the fuze. He tried to add more, but without success. Nevertheless he regarded the bomb as safe to move and it was taken by lorry to

Hampstead Heath bomb cemetery, where a remote fuze extractor was fitted. But when Carlyle tried to remove the fuze, again he was thwarted. The fuze refused to budge. Still believing the fuze to be safe, he decided to resort to brute force and a hammer, chisel and crowbar eventually liberated the fuze from the pocket. In this case, his ignorance of the situation was truly bliss.

As soon as the fuze was free Carlyle knew he was dealing with something new and entirely different. It was longer than a normal 25 fuze, and the cause of the difficult extraction was an anti-withdrawal device. The bottom of the fuze had an inverted taper and around it was a ring that slid down to increase the fuze's diameter and thereby prevent it being pulled out of the top of the fuze pocket. After removing the fuze's gaine to make it safe, he immediately took it to the administration research headquarters at Romney Street in London. Major John P. Hudson was stationed there, in charge of the experimental work and research into bomb disposal. Hudson himself had had experience in the field, and this was to be crucial to the development of a means of immunizing the Y fuze. Its discovery was a memorable event for Major Hudson.

I shall never forget the night when I was in my office. It was fairly late and I was rung by London Headquarters. I was told that a fuze of an entirely new type had been found by a chap called Carlyle and he was on his way in. I rang the Air Ministry and the Navy and their chaps came down straightaway. The Ministry of Supply man Bob Hurst was also there. The four of us were there sitting round my desk waiting for this chap to turn up with the fuze. It turned out to look superficially quite different to anything we had ever seen. On the top it looked exactly the same but the fuze itself was considerably longer and was in two parts. We had never seen anything like that before.

Well, what do you do? You take it apart and see what's inside. I suppose in hindsight we should have X-rayed it but we hadn't got the equipment there. We unscrewed it and found that it was obviously an electrical fuze that had something to do with heating, and if you did move it in any direction it would go off. And, from the outside, there was no reason to suppose that it wasn't just an ordinary 25 fuze. If you tried to pull it out or if you tried to twist it, or if you tried to take the bomb away with it in, it was bound to go off. Since [the bomb disposal officer] thought that it was a 'safe' fuze he wouldn't have taken any precautions in telling people what he was going to do or anything. He would just be blown up.

Now, if we had a report that night that poor old Carlyle had been killed, we would have said, 'Too bad.' Then the next night or the next day another destroyed the bomb disposal officer... how many times would that happen before we smelt a rat? It was a tremendous stroke of luck that the first one didn't go off.

The fuze itself was complex not least because it contained a dry battery rather than a capacitor as its power source. This meant that the fuze had the potential to explode until the battery was discharged, and that could be for a year or more. The top half of the fuze closely resembled a regular impact fuze. As it fell the fuze became armed and a trembler switch completed the circuit. But that is where the similarities ended. The first circuit did not fire the bomb: it merely completed a second circuit that was powered by the dry cell battery. That in turn was connected to the detonator. This circuit was completed by a series of three sensitive mercury tilt switches that were positioned at right angles to each other, together with a trembler switch similar to the one on the 50 fuze. All four switches were electrically in parallel. Thus after impact, any vibration or a slight movement of just two degrees or more in any direction would close one or more switches, thereby completing the firing circuit and resulting in the detonation of the bomb.

The Y fuze's complexity presented an enormous challenge. It was quickly discovered that the BD discharger, which forced liquid into the fuze head to neutralize it, would with the Y fuze merely serve to cause a short circuit in the dry cell battery – which could have explosive consequences. The bomb was one giant booby-trap designed to go off only when disturbed. Hudson and the team went to work immediately.

Within minutes those of us around the table could see that we had a new type of fuze; a brand new type of fuze, quite different to anything we had seen before. It was designed so that you couldn't pull it straight off the bomb; you could only get it out by turning it and if you twisted it in any direction, irrespective of the angle the bomb was lying, one or other of the three mercury switches was bound to flop across and make a contact which would set the bomb off.

Nobody could recall ever having seen a single letter Y marked alone on the head of a fuze. It took only hours for the warning to go out and be in the hands of every BD section in the country. No bomb that contained a fuze with the Y marking or indeed, any fuze that could not be safely identified, was to be worked on until further notice. Hudson also requested that all fuzes that had been recovered already should be looked at.

The first thing was to find out whether it was the Y that gave us the clue. The reasoning was that no matter what the fuze was supposed to do, the chap who saw it in the aeroplane must know what it is. Within the next few days we got everybody to look at all the fuzes they had. All bomb disposal units had masses of fuzes, including masses of 25s. We got them all to look at any of these fuzes and see if they could find a letter stamped on the top of any one. Within days we got literally thousands of descriptions of fuze heads; anybody who had a fuze looked at it. We got all the information together, sorted it to see whether there were any other permutations of markings. Of course nobody could find one. The only one that was totally different was the letter Y. This was the mark which seemed to identify this fuze as different from any other 25 that we had ever seen before.

But if the fuze was so dangerous, how did Captain Carlyle escape death? Hudson had his suspicions.

When we examined the fuze in detail we saw that there was one connection in the wiring which seemed rather iffy. We always assumed that that was why it didn't go off. Now, whether it was sabotage or just a bad manufacture, or whether they hadn't got a testing procedure, it escaped and Carlyle didn't get blown up. It was a colossal bid on the part of the German command bombers to catch the bomb disposers: the only time in the war that there was a deliberate attempt not just to interfere with the war effort, but to catch out bomb disposers. Here was the first time we had a fuze which was camouflaged to look like something 'safe'. Carlyle should have been killed.

There had not been many raids in the weeks leading up to January 1943. The raid, while not unexpected, was notable. German intelligence was good enough to know that Britain was dealing with a lot of bombs that did not go off. However, their intelligence was also telling them that the situation was under control. Casualty levels in bomb disposal were light and civilian morale was high. The fear among those in command was that morale in bomb disposal would be dented. If suddenly one bomb disposal officer after another were being killed for no apparent reason, then the natural inclination would be not to approach any bomb. The first thing Hudson and his team had to establish was how many of these Y fuzes were out there.

We had the fuze in our hand and we had to decide what to do about it. The first thing we did of course was to find out whether this was a one-off bomb or whether it was part of a stick of bombs. We soon found out through the regional commissioners that in fact a number of bombs, about thirteen or fourteen, had been dropped that night and this was one of them. None of the others had gone off. Of course, our assumption was that all the others in that stick were Y fuzes.

The race was now on to find a way of immunizing this new fuze. However, there was one bomb that could not wait. It had been dropped in the same raid as the Lord's Cricket Ground bomb and given category A1 status as it had fallen through the roof of a machine depot. Major C. A. J. Martin with Lieutenant R. W. Deans and his working party attended. Work began on the morning of 18 January. Hudson and his colleagues were still studying the first device but the bomb was in a difficult position and by the time Martin and Dean reached it, the initial findings were through. It was decided that a radiographic photograph should be taken. Obtaining such an image, similar to an X-ray, on such a volatile bomb was painstaking work. But after twelve hours a good image was produced.

The fuze was indeed identical to the one currently being scrutinized at Romney Street. It was decided that this fuze would have to be dealt with immediately, and Martin and Dean set about unscrewing the base plate. The bomb contained a solid TNT filling and work began to steam it out at midday on 20 January. This was a cumbersome procedure, and preventing any movement was not at all easy. It took until 8.30 a.m. the next day to complete the job, after a night during which Martin and Deans had taken turns lying under the bomb, surrounded by steam and the disgusting smell of molten TNT. Their immense bravery was to be rewarded. Martin received the George Cross and Deans the George Medal.

It had to be assumed that this was the beginning of a new wave and a new way of bombing. The implications were enormous. But it was not to be long before a breakthrough. Ironically, it was the sophisticated innovation of the fuze that was to be the weakest link. The dry cell battery gave Bob Hurst, the scientist from the Ministry of Supply, the vital clue. Like all batteries, it was susceptible to the cold. The answer had to be in cooling the fuze. But, bearing in mind that moving the bomb was impossible, how could the fuze be cooled sufficiently without removing it from the bomb? Hudson explains:

> *No technique that we had such as the magnetic clock-stopper was going to be any use at all. Here we had something that was activated by a battery that might last as long as any flashlight battery; a year perhaps, there was no time limit. Bob Hurst said, well, could we inactivate it by cooling it? We went and got a flashlight battery and we happened to have some liquid oxygen. We put two wires on to the electric battery and dropped it in. Of course, after a few seconds its output just fell off to nothing. We tried with the Y fuze batteries and the same applied. So if we could cool those batteries down to a temperature below a certain level then we could assume the battery was dead and we could pull the fuze out, even if it meant rotating it.*

The solution had been found. Oxygen becomes liquid at 219 degrees below zero and as such would lower the temperature of the metal bomb case, fuze and batteries sufficiently to make them lose their charge. The next problem was how to apply it out in the field. The batteries were in a fuze that was in turn in a fuze pocket encased within a steel case containing 500 kilograms of high explosive. Not only did it make freezing the batteries extremely difficult, it was impossible to attach any means of reading the electrical output of the batteries within a fuze that was still inside a bomb. How would they know if the fuze was cold enough? The liquid oxygen provided the key.

They attached wires to the batteries which were used to read the electrical output. Then the fuze was reinserted into the fuze pocket. Initial experiments involved slowly dripping liquid oxygen on to the fuze head. The difficult thing to determine was how long the dripping needed to continue. A surprisingly simple solution was quickly discovered: 'We noticed as we were doing this that as the bomb got colder that a ring of frost started to develop round the fuze head, and as we kept on dripping the oxygen this patch got bigger and bigger.'

The ring of frost had a diameter of 20 inches (50 centimetres) but a more rigorous method of assessing the temperature was needed. Measuring the ring was not an accurate measure of temperature because a number of factors influenced the amount of frost, not least the amount of humidity in the atmosphere. Thermometers were not practical. One of the team came up with the idea of attaching small strips of wet cotton wool at 1-inch (2.5-centimetre) intervals, starting at the fuze and radiating outwards. Once twenty of the little strips had frozen and stuck to the bomb casing then the locking ring could be undone, twisted and the fuze pulled out. But Hudson and the team realized the limitations to this procedure. Liquid oxygen was not the easiest of chemicals to use in this situation. Hudson got the chance to try out the invention of 24 January, only five days after the first bomb had dropped.

That [method] was wonderful when we got a bomb lying with the fuze at the top but if the fuze was at the side, it wasn't quite so easy. Fortunately we never had one with the fuze right at the bottom. I think it must have been me who thought of the idea of making a little neck of clay around the side to hold the liquid. I think I used plasticine actually. I did the one which was waiting at Albert Bridge. It was a Sunday afternoon, a lovely day, and I went down to do this job with Bob Hurst and the arrangement was that we made this little cup, poured the stuff in and measured the diameter of hoarfrost. I poured some in and then it took a few seconds to fizzle away. Bob came and did it once, which as a civilian he shouldn't have done, but he said he'd like to be able to say he did one of these.

Eventually the fuze seemed to be inert. It was time to remove it. By this time, Hudson had an audience. London was split into two areas – north and south – and their respective colonels had arrived as well as Brigadier H. H. Bateman, who was in charge of all bomb disposals in the London area.

After freezing, it was estimated that there was about twenty minutes during which time the fuze could be extracted safely. The first thing was to remove a locking ring and use a steel bar through a ring attached to the fuze head to twist and loosen it. Once twisted loose, a piece of string was attached and Hudson retired to a safe distance: 'I had got a brigadier and two colonels at a safe distance behind a sort of wall. When the time came to pull the string I was going to pull it gently. But these colonels wanted to have a bit of the action so the three chaps pulled and they all went down on their arses because the string broke!' Hudson had no option but to go back in and pull the fuze out by hand.

The successful operation had taken twenty-three minutes from beginning to end. Over the next few days, Hudson developed a new means of delivering the liquid oxygen via a brass container, and went on to deal with another bomb. Details of the new technique were circulated immediately to bomb disposal section all over the country. However, there were still more than a dozen bombs to deal with and this was by Hudson's own admission, a 'rough and ready' method. Nevertheless, it was the best available and Captain Carlyle was one of the officers who were charged with its use. He attended another bomb with a Y fuze, along with Major Martin, who had bravely defuzed the bomb in the machine depot. This time they were using the newly developed immunizing technique. Another officer, Montague Bool, would normally have dealt with the bomb as it had fallen in his patch. He had been given the nickname 'Ferdy' after the popular cartoon bull of the time. Ferdy Bool was with Carlyle and Martin at the bombsite and describes the scene:

It was a bomb that I would normally have dealt with but because the equipment had not yet been issued to units it was only in the hands of the specialist team who had dealt with the first bombs to be discovered. Carlyle had a magnetic stethoscope which he could put on his neck to replay sound to the headphones. Major Martin was in the background at the listening post. Major Martin asked if I would go and see how [Carlyle] was getting on. I was walking down from the listening post to the bomb, which was in a sort of wooden outbuilding. When I was a few paces from the bomb, Carlyle came rushing out in great pain, shouting at the top of his voice, 'Keep away! Keep away!' A fire had started while he was working on the bomb and he obviously thought there was a danger of the heat of the fires neutralizing the freezing process and perhaps the bomb going up.

Major Martin came up to see what was happening and decided that the best thing would be if I took Carlyle to the hospital. [Martin] would put out the fire and deal with the bomb. I took him to a first aid post but they said the burns were much too serious for them. He'd have to go straight to hospital.

The burns were indeed serious and Carlyle was kept in hospital for more than a month. Martin managed to get the fire under control. Fortunately it had not taken hold and only some of the surrounding woodwork was alight. The fuze had to be refrozen and the immunization was completed successfully. The incident raised some serious issues and led to the re-evaluation of the way in which the liquid oxygen was used. It would appear that on this occasion the liquid oxygen, which is highly flammable, had spontaneously combusted in a poorly ventilated out-house. Major Hudson's insulated brass container was developed and issued to the bomb disposal companies. The new container had a valve to prevent the natural build-up of pressure.

Remarkably, all the secrets of the Y fuze had been uncovered within a week of the first bomb falling. The final stage in the conquest of the fuze came when an alternative to liquid oxygen was discovered. As has been shown, liquid oxygen can be dangerous to handle and was not always readily available. Carbon dioxide, however, was available. It was discovered that if compressed carbon dioxide was released from its cylinder into a standard army kit bag, it formed a substance known as carbon dioxide snow. Mixed with methylated spirit, this formed a perfect freezing compound which, packed around a Y fuze head, would produce a drop in temperature sufficient to neutralize the fuze.

Bombs containing these fuzes continued to fall for over a year. Although Major Hudson thought the fuzes may well have been experiments by 'German boffins', he was still concerned by the possibilities they created:

I have often wondered about German High Command, who must have been told what was going on. Somebody must have authorized the use of these fuzes. Having done so, they would keep their eyes glued to the network of intelligence they had, to hear whether any bombs had been going off in London. And they'd say, 'Well, yes, there was one actually. Just a single bomber and he dropped a few but none of them went off, but one did go off the next day and another the next.' That would tell the German High Command that we were trying to deal with them, we had tumbled them and we were getting killed.

Suppose that had happened. Would we have taken [everyone] off bomb disposal? Would we say we're not going to do it? I have no idea what would have happened.

8

Butterflies over Grimsby

*Huge numbers of bombs had been dropped. They were every-
where: cinema projection rooms, gutters, hedges, sewers. If you
could think of a place, there was a bomb there.*

COLONEL ERIC WAKELING RE

THE NORTH SEA PORT OF GRIMSBY is more readily associated with
fish than insects with colourful wings. But these particular butterflies,
which descended on the town in June 1943, were an altogether
different species: inanimate – and deadly. They were responsible for
the worst night in Grimsby's history.

The 92,000 inhabitants of Grimsby and the nearby resort town of
Cleethorpes had been used to bombing, and the raid on the night of
13 June, although heavy, did not seem to be unusual. The busy port at
the bottom of the Humber estuary had been in the bombing equivalent of a rain shadow as the Luftwaffe had focused the majority of their
ordnance on Hull, a stone's throw to the north. By 1943 the docks
were to all intents and purposes being run by the Admiralty, vital for
repairs and stores for minesweepers, of which many were requisitioned from Grimsby's trawler fleet. The town's position on the North
Sea had made it a major fishing port for centuries, and fish was a vital
source of protein for people whose wartime weekly meat ration would
not fill the inside of a takeaway hamburger today.

The town's strong manufacturing base, which went hand-in-hand with its role as a port, was now being directed towards building lorries and transport for thousands of American troops billeted in the area. The vehicle components were shipped from the States in crates. This concentration of men and materials, concluded a later Home Office report, must have been misinterpreted by the Germans as preparations for the embarkation of troops to Europe – preparations they would want to delay. In fact, the large numbers of troops and heavy materials were being prepared for other manoeuvres, far in advance of preparations for D-Day.

There had not been a serious raid since August 1942. Another summer had arrived, and people started to relax – perhaps becoming a little blasé. Could the worst be over? In fact the worst was to come: within the space of forty-eight hours there would be sixty-six people dead and hundreds more maimed and injured.

Pat Beaumont was an eleven-year-old girl living in Warneford Avenue, Cleethorpes, in June 1943. Pat and her mother and grandmother were crammed into the cupboard under the stairs along with Mrs Westerbury from next door and half a dozen relatives from Wigan. Her memories of sitting on Mrs Westerbury's knocking knees are still vivid.

It seemed to happen so quickly this particular night. We didn't have a chance to get into the air-raid shelter. Our relations from Wigan had never experienced an air raid and they were scared to death. There was all this noise going on but you know, I can't ever remember feeling frightened at all. There was my gran – she was one of these characters – and we kept hearing these big explosions and glass breaking, and all of a sudden there was a big bang and I said, 'Gran, that's all our windows gone in!' 'Shut up! Shut up!' she said, pulling a face at me, because she didn't want to frighten all the relations from Wigan.

Moments later, still unable to keep quiet, Pat exclaimed to the still terrified relatives from Wigan that she could smell smoke. The incendiaries were doing their work. The town was ablaze. Pat's recollections reflect the Luftwaffe bombing strategy that night of 13 June: it was a fine evening with no wind and a three-quarters-full moon. The first pass of twenty-three enemy aircraft dropped the flares and incendiaries, lighting up the town to make a clear target for the bombers. Next, the planes re-circled and, with the town alight below them, dropped 18 tonnes of high explosive bombs over the two towns. By now the fire service and civil defence personnel, so vital to the preservation of the already smouldering town, were rushing to their posts and assessing which fires and bombed houses to go to first.

Once the civil defence staff were all drawn out into the open, the planes returned to drop their final load: the SD2s. These were the butterfly bombs, so called because of their shape. They rained down in their thousands: 2-kilogram (4.5-pound) parcels primed to maim, kill and cause terror. They targeted not only the civil defence personnel but all the men, women and children who would leave their shelters in the belief that it was safe to do so, the planes having left and the all-clear sounding. Butterfly bombs killed fourteen people during the raid. In the two hours after the all-clear sounded, a further forty-three people lost their lives. And this was by no means the last of the casualties that would result from that night.

Although it weighed 2 kilograms, the butterfly bomb (or SD2 anti-personnel bomb, to give its correct ordnance title), contained only 225 grams of high explosive. The explosive weighed less than the average pack of butter but the damage it could do was staggering. A person standing within 25 metres (80 feet) of an exploding SD2 would almost certainly be killed; while the shrapnel radius of 150 metres (nearly 500 feet) presented a serious risk of injury leading to death.

The first reports of these bombs being used in Britain goes back as far as October 1940, when a number were dropped around Ipswich in Suffolk, both on the town and on nearby RAF Wattisham. No. 8 section of 4 Company Bomb Disposal would deal with the bombs in town, while the RAF would deal with those on their own ground. But before the Royal Engineers could arrive, several police officers who had unwittingly handled the devices had lost their lives. It did not take long for the RE officer in charge to realize that this was a new type of bomb; and with great bravery, the section sergeant unscrewed the arming mechanism of one 'dud' bomb and removed the fuze. Its recovery and subsequent examination were to provide valuable help in Grimsby nearly three years later. At the time, the incident was overshadowed by the heavy raids of much larger bombs then being experienced.

The butterfly bomb was ideal for use over airfields. John Henry was an airman stationed at RAF Wattisham when the daylight raid occurred. A high explosive bomb had brought the roof down on the barracks occupied by aircrew, and Henry's room orderly was in that section of the barracks at the time. The bomb had been destined for the airmen's side but had deflected off the ground. Henry remembers the orderly well: 'He was a very nice lad. He was always in our place very early in the morning but that day he was late. He had his head blown off. I saw him carried out. It was terrible. It was later that we discovered these butterfly bombs had been dropped all over the airfield.'

The grass runway was littered with them, buried everywhere in the thick grass. Flying was immediately cancelled. Every available man was assembled, given a bundle of sticks and told to mark any bombs they found that had not exploded. Strict instructions were given not to touch them. When this exercise had been completed the RAF armourers went out with their vans to collect them. Henry remembers: 'We had two sergeant armourers killed. I saw one while I was standing by the control tower and saw this chap by the van with his stomach blown out.'

The devastation and confusion experienced by Wattisham prefigured what Grimsby was to endure three years later. One of the biggest problems in dealing with the butterfly bomb was that it looked more interesting than deadly; it did not conform to the common perceptions of what a bomb should look like and, despite warnings about not touching anything unfamiliar, its strange appearance aroused the curiosity in many unfortunate people. The body of the bomb itself was cylindrical and made of cast iron with the approximate height and diameter of a small can of baked beans. Before it was armed, the body was encased in a light steel jacket, the two halves of which cupped the bomb and attached to the spindle of the fuze by a 15-centimetre (6-inch) steel cable. The fuze itself was in a small pocket in the side of the bomb body.

The bombs were packed in batches of twenty-three into cylinders and loaded aboard aircraft. When this cylinder was dropped, it opened at a pre-set height, releasing the individual bombs. The pressure of falling forced the two jacket halves to open away from the body of the bomb and act like small wings, slowing its descent. As the wings worked their way over the arming spindle and up the steel cable, in conjunction with another two small rotating wings, the bomb spun its way to earth while turning the spindle to arm the fuze.

But, by 1943 the bomb had been redesigned and included new methods of detonation. There were now three different kinds of fuzes used in the SD2s. The first (number 41) was designed to go off on impact or within seconds of hitting the ground. The second (number 67) had a clockwork delay action that could be set to function up to thirty minutes after impact. The third (number 70) was the most deadly: a simple mechanical fuze, it was partly armed during its fall to earth. When it impacted, a trip switch allowed the mechanism to run for a further five seconds to allow it to fully arm. Thereafter the slightest movement would trigger the fuze to detonate the bomb.

Despite the wings acting like brakes, the bombs still fell at considerable speed, allowing them to penetrate through roofs and into buildings but not deep into the ground like a standard high explosive bomb. Butterfly bombs were small enough to be hidden in hedges and fields and a myriad other hard-to-reach and unexpected places.

At the heart of events in Grimsby on that night of 13/14 June was the Air Raid Precaution report centre in the basement of the town's municipal offices. At one stage, messages were arriving at the centre at a rate of one every six seconds. It had all started at 1.29 a.m. when the 'red alert' was sounded. A huge formation of bombers had been picked up by the RAF heading up the Humber estuary. There were a number of possible targets in the area – Hull being the most likely. However, it was not long before the 'red alert' had been upgraded to 'Immediate Danger'. The target was definitely Grimsby.

Joyce Farthing worked in the report centre. She was not supposed to be on duty that night, but as she did shorthand she would be needed; she got a call that the local alderman would be coming by to pick her up and take her into the town hall. She recalls: 'The raid was on as we drove along Doughty Road towards the town hall. I can remember seeing all these little things fluttering to earth like confetti. It was only later that I realized how lucky we were not to be hit by any. We got to the report centre and it was chaos.'

The first UXB was found in the back yard of a house in the centre of Grimsby. The reported time was 2.17 a.m. and it was followed by hundreds of similar calls over the next day and a half. By 2.56 a.m., amid the many reports of incendiaries – which had set much of the town including the paper mill alight – it was known that the hundreds of UXBs were the anti-personnel devices also known as butterfly bombs.

As the all-clear sounded, people emerged from their homes and Anderson shelters to see the wholesale devastation wrought by high explosive bombs and incendiaries. The fish docks, so vital to the local economy and the health of the nation, were ablaze, as were hundreds of houses and public buildings. As people struggled through the streets in the dark, they were confronted by yet another horror: the SD2. What were these curious-shaped metal objects hanging from clotheslines, lodged in trees and attached to railings? They were everywhere: strange little tin cans with wings on top. Stumbling through the darkness, some people lost limbs while others were blinded, and as ambulances and fire engines drove over the bombs they were wrecked.

Vernon Godwin was in his late teens and had spent the night in the air-raid shelter with his sister. He remembers looking out and seeing the flares. His father, who was the chief air-raid warden for the district, came in just after the raid was over. He told Vernon that he thought there must be a lot of UXBs as there were craters everywhere. In fact – and confusingly – when the SD2s exploded they left a small crater that looked suspiciously like the entry hole for a conventional bomb. The ones that exploded on impact were designed only to scare people. It was those that did not go off which were to cause the most problems – and Vernon's night was only just beginning, as he describes.

We had the job of charging batteries on lorries that were being assembled at Cleethorpes and we had a lot of sulphuric acid stored at the factory. I really wanted to go and see that they were okay. My friend David wanted to go and see his father who was in charge of civilian war dead. At that time, we'd no idea that anybody had been killed. We walked from our house to Victoria Street and checked everything was okay [at the factory]. There was a bus outside. It had one of these [butterfly] bombs in it and was protected by sandbags...

As we walked into King Edward Street David's father got hold of us and said, 'Come on. There are some bodies to collect at the central market.' At the corner of the central market, there was the old Salvation Army hostel and all the old chaps out of there went into the shelter while the raid was on. Of course, unaware, they came out of the shelter and stumbled on these bombs... They'd no chance of avoiding them, even if they'd known they were there. It just blew half of them away. Anyway, David and I, we had a handcart and we loaded these bodies on to the handcart and took them to the morgue.

Vernon also remembers the rather macabre way in which one police officer sought to warn people of the damage these bombs could do: 'There was a policeman on duty at the box in the central market and he said there had been people round looking for souvenirs. He said to one of them, 'Here you are,' and dropped somebody's thumb into their hand.'

Meanwhile, the Civil Defence Regional Headquarters had called the Royal Engineers: 3 Company Bomb Disposal had recently been brought together in Tollerton Hall, near Nottingham. It was unusual for a whole company to be together in one place; outside the major metropolitan areas, the individual sections making up a company were often billeted far apart from each other. The men had just began to enjoy their camaraderie and congenial surroundings, naturally unaware of the magnitude of the task ahead of them.

The message had come through at 3 a.m., and the company commander, Major W. G. Parker, decided to send his three most experienced officers to the scene immediately. At this point only a few reports had trickled in and most UXBs seemed to be on the surface. The three drove eastwards through the night.

Dawn was breaking as they drove into town and with the light came relative safety. The bombs littered the streets and those that had been moved, or driven or cycled over, had already had fatal consequences. Several police officers, members of the public and civil defence staff had already been killed in the hours of darkness, so easily hidden were the butterfly bombs.

Dick Bridge was then a 28-year-old Special Policeman awaiting call-up into the RAF. This had been deferred as he was in charge of local authority pumping stations in the area. He remembers being called out when the siren went and trying to manoeuvre through the streets in darkness. His orders were to head for the residential area of Nunsthorpe.

As I was approaching Nunsthorpe I could hear the bombs going off and later I could see the fire coming out of the roofs and guttering, which in those days were wood. I went to the point and the sergeant told me to walk down Sutcliffe Avenue. As I walked down the avenue I could see these little things in the gutters and the gardens. Nunsthorpe was absolutely saturated with them. As I got further down the avenue, I saw two chaps who were obviously dead. I found out later they had picked one of these bombs up. Curiosity had got the better of them. It killed both of them on the spot...

There was a lot of screaming coming from some of the houses. People had found their loved ones killed in the back gardens. I was told to be aware of anybody coming out of their houses, anybody walking on the footpath. I also had to watch out for dogs... many of them escaped. I had to be careful of these two dead chaps on the side of the road, and make sure no dogs went round there.

It quickly became apparent to all concerned that there was an immense amount of work to be done. The three officers from No. 3 Company Bomb Disposal found their way to the central police station where there was an atmosphere of barely controlled chaos. One of the three officers, Lieutenant Clifford Green, cast an eye over the situation and recommended that a dedicated 'war room' be set up immediately to co-ordinate what was, by this time, clearly going to be a very long and complex operation. There was no way that three officers were going to be able to deal with an incident of this magnitude on their own. Green telephoned Major Parker who, on hearing of the scale of the problem, dispatched every officer and sergeant and one complete section to the area. By 5 a.m. Grimsby and Cleethorpes had been declared one large Category A2 incident. The towns were paralyzed. As daylight came, the scale of the problem became even more apparent. Dick Bridge remembers what happened in one street that morning.

As daylight approached [in Sutcliffe Avenue] the people in many of the houses had to go to work. The women fortunately walked in the middle of the footpath, but the chaps had bicycles and it was my job to shout out from one end of the road to stop these fellas pushing their bikes any further than their gates. I pointed out to them what lay ahead in the middle of the road. They diligently approached the gutters and had a good look at these things and then they had to walk, not cycle, down the middle of

*the road until they reached the main road, which was compara-
tively clear. I will say this, they obeyed my instructions and I
don't think I heard of anybody being killed through going into
the gutters or kicking one.*

Sadly, he was not able to prevent his own uncle from becoming a
victim. Later that day Albert Bridge was hit by shrapnel outside 17
Sutcliffe Avenue. An inspector in the Grimsby Constabulary, he lived
in the village of Great Coates and had enjoyed the day spent at his
grandson's christening. When the raid started he made his way to his
post. As he was walking along Sutcliffe Avenue with his colleague, PC
Walter Rouse, a young sailor had kicked a butterfly bomb in a garden.
The sailor was killed instantly but the shrapnel hit Inspector Bridge in
the legs and head, just below the rim of his helmet. PC Rouse was also
hit, blowing his leg off and causing severe internal injuries. Both men
died in hospital of their wounds.

Eric Wakeling, last seen in action in Chapter 2, was by now a 23-
year-old lieutenant with 3 Company Bomb Disposal. He had drawn the
short straw and on arriving in Grimsby he had had to deal with the
high explosive UXBs which were also hampering the town. He arrived
a little later in the day, having made slower progress than the other
officers who had raced to the scene without their sections: 'I arrived
at the police headquarters and found only one officer on duty. It had
been decided that only one officer would man the station and they
were taking it in turns. Nobody wanted to miss the fun.'

The 'war room' was staffed by police officers and was dominated by
two maps. The first was a street map of Grimsby covered in different-
coloured pins. The second was an Ordnance Survey map of the
surrounding area, which in the weeks to come was also to become
covered with pins, as organized searches of the more rural areas got
under way. Each pin represented a reported bomb and policewomen
kept a numbered log of each reported incident. These were then
transcribed on to cards and handed out in location-related groupings as
officers returned for more reports. As the cards relating to the bombs

that had been dealt with were handed back, slowly and surely the pins on the boards changed colour, indicating 'cleared' bombs.

As the officers returned and reported on the jobs they had done, it became clear that the fuzing of the bombs was proving to be a problem. Two of the fuzes were new to the bomb disposal officers and the 67 – designed with a time delay, exploding anything up to thirty minutes after the bomb had landed – was proving especially tricky. Many of them seemed to be suffering from a manufacturing fault, which caused the clockwork mechanism to jam just before they were due to go off. Nobody ever found out how long that delay might have been. The type 70 fuze was a pure anti-handling device, which had cost so many lives and injured so many and was proving to be just as problematic. The slightest vibration was causing them to explode, so even approaching them to lay sandbags was incurring a considerable risk.

By 17 June a delegation from the Home Office had arrived in Grimsby to assess the problems and gauge what to expect should the raid be repeated elsewhere. It was noted with some surprise that despite three dozen RE officers and men being on site and working flat out dealing with the bombs that were being reported, no organized search had yet been started. The maps covered in coloured pins represented bombs that had been reported by the public. Without a methodical search it was impossible to guage how many more there might be. It was recommended that the Fire Service and ARP should undertake this work immediately.

Pat Beaumont remembers playing in her garden when an ARP officer arrived a few days after the raid. Doreen, her next-door neighbour who had been injured by a butterfly bomb, had only just returned home from hospital.

Gran was [in the house] and I went and fetched her out. He walked her down to the bottom of the garden and he said, 'You see that hole in your roof, don't you? I'm afraid you've got a bomb in it. If I was you, I wouldn't use that bedroom.'

Well, Doreen was actually laid in the bedroom on their side, so they had to take her out. They had to bung up all the fireplaces, bring the bedding down and sleep on the floor in the front room because we couldn't use the bedrooms. We went to the Conservative Club in Cleethorpes on the day they exploded it.

We eventually got the windows put back in and the ceiling done... I thought it was great fun. Ours were the only two houses in the street that it had happened to, you see. Nobody else had got a bomb in the roof. I think you were a little bit proud of it!

Even the countryside surrounding Grimsby was not to be immune. Curious cows were being killed and injured by the bombs. The death of these beasts was especially galling in a time of such severe meat shortage – all the dead and destroyed animals had to go to the knacker's yard; not being slaughtered in an abattoir, they were deemed unfit for human consumption. Crossing fields to reach the dead and dying animals was especially treacherous – the small black bombs were easily hidden in the grass.

It was crucial to spread the word about just how dangerous these bombs could be. But there was an intrinsic problem in this: news of the effects of the raid had to be kept out of the press. If the Germans realized how successful the raid had been, there was nothing to stop them repeating it on an even more densely populated town or city. Word of mouth and the efficiency of the air raid wardens seemed to be the only way. There were, however, even more graphic warnings given to the public. At the base of the clock tower in Grimsby's Central Market, a display of butterfly bombs had been laid out along with large posters warning people not to touch or move them. In addition, there was a boot placed next to one of the bombs, within which its unfortunate owner's foot remained.

The officers and NCOs of No. 3 Company had more than enough work to go round. At this point the orders were to dispose of all SD2s in situ. There was no way of knowing if the type 67 fuzes were ticking or if they had jammed how long they had to run, and the type 70s could not be moved without exploding them anyway. This was not a problem when the bombs lay on open ground or in the street. A circle of sandbags could be built around the bomb and a slab of gun cotton used to detonate it. However, this began to get very expensive on sandbags as the explosion blew most of them apart. Over 27,000 were used over the course of clearing Grimsby of bombs. Of course the sand could be used again, but it needed men to collect it and fill more sandbags.

One bright subaltern had the ingenious idea of using straw bales. Not only did they absorb the explosion even better than sand, but they could also be used again. The other advantage was that the walls surrounding the bombs could be built much more quickly.

The problems, however, became much more severe when the bombs were inside people's homes. Lieutenant Wakeling had finished the work he had to do on the high explosive bombs and began to help with the numerous butterfly bombs.

We were just causing so much damage to property so we decided to formulate our own plans. I remember my first bomb was on the floor of a very prettily decorated pink bedroom. It was obviously a woman's room. I don't know if she was married, but it impressed me and I thought, what can I do to save this room. The bomb had a type 70 (anti-disturbance) fuze so Maggs, my batman, and I tiptoed round the bomb creating a nest of sandbags to insulate the bomb. I then unwound a length of string and, making a loop in one end, placed it over the wings of the bomb. We laid a board over the top and covered it with sandbags to further insulate the blast, and retired down the stairs and into the garden.

I took in the slack and positioned myself against the wall between the two downstairs windows. I gave it a short sharp tug and was somewhat astonished when the two windows on either side of me blew out. It would seem that I had protected the bedroom all right but succeeded in deflecting the blast down the way through the floor with enough force to blow out the downstairs windows.

Still, the bedroom remained pretty in pink. Had it been a type 67 fuze, there would not have been any time to make the elaborate arrangements necessary, and adding a 1lb slab of gun cotton would have in effect doubled the force of the blast. Was there any other way that the butterfly bombs fitted with time delay fuzes could be dealt with? Once again a subaltern came up with a solution. It involved a system of pulleys and some calculated risk-taking. A hook would be attached to the window frame of the room in which the bomb was found. A piece of string would be threaded through the hook and tied to the bomb. From a distance the bomb would then be pulled into the window frame where a second string would pull it clear of the house. When the first string was released, the bomb would drop on to a nest of sandbags in the garden below, there to explode.

Wakeling and his team successfully cleared a number of houses with no damage using this method, a fact of which he is justifiably proud to this day. It should be noted that although successful, this technique carried with it a significant risk. In his desire to preserve the property of the people of Grimsby, he and his men could have suffered severe injury or even death had one of the bombs exploded before it dropped into the garden.

It may seem strange that the desire to preserve domestic property seemed to be edging out the more sensible regard for the lives of the officers involved, but there was more than the issue of morale at stake. Given that the Germans must not know how effective their weapon was, it was vital that any message they did receive would be that it had failed in its mission. Destruction had been minimal and, despite not being the first raid on a civilian area by such a frightening weapon, the concentration and numbers used were unprecedented. It was only the speed and effectiveness of the bomb disposal teams that prevented what would otherwise have been long-term chaos.

It was not just domestic premises that were affected by the butterfly bombs. Lieutenant Wakeling's next mission was to examine a coal yard. It had sidings, which ran into the lines of the main Grimsby station, and on them were a number of coal trucks, some full and some empty. The number of bombs in the coal yard was as yet unknown and Lieutenant Wakeling and his batman Maggs set about finding out how many were going to have to be disposed of. Slowly, they worked their way along the lines of wagons. If it contained a bomb the wagon was marked with a chalk cross. It was just not possible to check each bomb to see what type of fuze it held. By their nature, the bombs were hard to spot in the trucks full of black coal. After an hour's searching, it appeared that there were nine bombs.

Lieutenant Wakeling decided to deal with those that lay on the coal in the full wagons. While hoping that all the bombs would have type 70 fuzes, he set about making loops of string, attaching a strong wire hook to the end of each. His plan was to retreat to a distance, having first thrown the string over part of the bomb. With this acting like a grappling hook, he hoped to then pull on the string and explode the bomb. This was easier planned than done. It was essential to throw the hook accurately, and it took a little practice to get the hooks into position. On the third attempt the bomb exploded. The second and third bombs were dealt with in a similar way. The remaining six in the empty coal wagons were to require yet more lateral thinking.

Understandably, Lieutenant Wakeling was not entirely happy at the prospect of jumping into coal wagons in which the only other occupant was a butterfly bomb primed to explode at the slightest movement. There was no way he could get close enough to attach his hook and string. His next plan required a trip to the stationmaster, who was leading a solitary watch as most of his men had disappeared. Wakeling proposed that the first wagon, which did not contain a bomb, be unhooked and used to act as a battering ram against the others, the force of which would (he hoped) detonate the remaining bombs.

Only four men were needed to move the wagon into position. The stationmaster rounded up two other helpers for Wakeling and Maggs, and the plan began to take shape. They unhooked the wagon and pushed it up the track towards the points. The brake was then applied and the men moved to the other side to push the battering-ram wagon back down the tracks towards its bomb-laden friends. As the wagon gained speed and neared the other wagons, the men all threw themselves to the ground and waited for the anticipated six explosions. There were only three, which thankfully did not injure any of those present.

This left Wakeling to deal with the remaining three. He decided to wait for half an hour and this patience paid off, partially. There was one more explosion. Hoping that this meant the other two were duds, with immense courage he entered the two remaining wagons armed with two slabs of gun cotton, primed and fitted with detonators. He placed each beside the remaining bombs, returned to the safe point, attached the wires to the exploder, depressed the plunger and delighted in the two simultaneous explosions.

It was to take nearly a week to clear all the reported butterfly bombs. In total 2,250 were dealt with, which is estimated to be an astonishing 60 per cent of all those that fell. Over 350 alone were dealt with on the last day of the week following the raid. Many more would turn up in the weeks, months and even years to come. Following the broadcast of the ITV drama *Danger UXB* in 1978, several butterfly bombs had to be dealt with by bomb disposal squads. One gamekeeper had been wondering for years about the funny metal object hanging from a tree in the wood he patrolled.

When it was deemed appropriate to scale down the operation, Eric Wakeling's section was detailed to remain in the area. There were still bombs to be dealt with in other locations and it was with a slightly heavy heart that the young lieutenant watched his fellow officers depart for their individual section HQs. But he knew there was still a job to do and he soon picked up his next report, which related to six butterfly bombs that had been located in a field of beans.

The farmer had very thoughtfully marked the location of each bomb with a 2-foot (60-centimetre) high stick. Unfortunately, by the time

Lieutenant Wakeling made it to the field several weeks after the first report the sticks were of little use as the beans were 3 feet high (nearly a metre). He and Maggs trekked through the field for nearly an hour and eventually found all six. There were three bombs fitted with type 67 fuzes and three with 70s. The men set about blowing up the type 67s in the hope that they would set off the rest. Accordingly, all the 67s were 'looped' with string and blown up, sympathetically exploding one of the 70s. The remaining two 70s were dealt with similarly, but an unexpected third explosion almost blew Wakeling and his batman off their feet.

In all another four UXBs were later found in the field and Wakeling has pondered for a long time on how lucky he and Maggs were to have survived while wandering through that field on that afternoon.

Their close shaves with death were not at an end, however. The next UXB they were detailed to attend was also on a farm. It had been a very stressful and tiring time and Lieutenant Wakeling decided that instead of checking all the fuzes in advance he would work his way through the field of cabbages, dealing with the bombs as they appeared. Again there were six bombs reported; five, which all had type 70 fuzes, were dealt with by attaching the string and pulling it. Number six proved a sticker and, suspecting that it had lodged behind a cabbage, Wakeling got up to investigate. A few yards away there was a huge bang. His guardian angel must have been on overtime – his head had not quite made it over the edge of the ditch in which he and Maggs were sheltering.

In the days and weeks that followed, a substantial amount of information was gathered to assess the impact of this raid and to try and learn some lessons from it. A Home Office report written some time after the raid conceded that a figure of '242 casualties is rather heavy, but quite a number of people have been made casualties since the raid through handling SD2 bombs.' It offered no further advice on how perhaps such heavy casualties could have been avoided; indeed, there has been conflicting accounts of the exact number of people who were killed in that raid. A Home Office memo from the time stored at the North East Lincolnshire Archive shows that there was not a little discomfort at the level of ignorance of the SD2, its appearance and effects. The Control Centre report on the attack stated:

It is noteworthy that UXAPBs [unexploded anti-personnel bombs] were being reported by one Warden's Division virtually during the raid as a message was received to this effect in the [Report Centre] at 0217. This is no doubt due to the fact that following HSC 76/43 full publicity as to these weapons was given to the Civil Defence Services in Grimsby on 7 May 1943, all the literature, including the illustration, being distributed.

The HSC 76/43 memo is still lodged with the archive. It consists of a small flyer about 20 x 30 centimetres (8 x 12 inches), warning people not to touch or go near the SD2 bomb that is clearly depicted. Unfortunately, there is no evidence that this memo was ever reproduced in any numbers or distributed to the relevant personnel of Grimsby. The Report of the Civil Defence Wardens took a slightly different view on the success of the operation. It included the views of the Head Warden, Rev Howard of Division 9, an area of Grimsby that was literally 'peppered' with anti-personnel/butterfly bombs. While being proud of all the workers his report stated: 'It is felt that the public had not been sufficiently informed of the dangers of the APBs [anti-personnel bombs] prior to the raid.'

Dick Bridge is prepared to go even further in his assessment of the level of information disseminated to the Civil Defence and the public.

Now I was involved in many of these operations and I can quite honestly say I never saw a leaflet. You can take it from me, there were no posters in my point where I was doing duty. If you look at it logically, had they known what these things were, would they have kicked them, would they have picked them up? They would have avoided them like the plague. They may have stuck some up in the town hall, the councillors may have known something about them... but when you get down to the nitty-gritty, the people who were going to be involved, what about them? I don't think anybody knew the dangers or what [butterfly bombs] looked like.

One of the most remarkable facts to come to light about this period in the history of Grimsby and Cleethorpes was the success in keeping the whole incident secret. It has been speculated that it was due to the lack of publicity the bombing received; the enemy never did fully appreciate the devastating effect that it could have had. It was also by a stroke of great luck that an entire BD company was within a couple of hours' drive. Arguably, had the Germans known the true potential of the bombs, they could have raided the south coast where the army was massing in preparation for D-Day.

Further attacks were anticipated and a massive training programme was undertaken in an effort to prepare. On the advice of Brigadier Bateman, 70,000 posters were printed, training films were made and distributed in their hundreds, trailers were shown in cinemas and radio broadcasts were made. It was recommended that torches should be used and headlights restored to avoid the unnecessary deaths that had resulted from people in the blackout unable to see the devices that lay in their paths. However, further attacks involving bombing of this concentration did not take place and mercifully the paralysis and destruction experienced in Lincolnshire was never to be repeated. The Germans dropped only another 11,000, over a wide area including London, Kent, Sussex and Essex as well as various RAF stations and Army camps.

There can be little doubt, though, that the Germans knew of the power of these bombs against military formations. They had been used extensively against the Red Army, where soldiers were reduced to dealing with them by shooting at them. No doubt the strategists had considered the effects of having to deal with one's own butterfly bombs in areas which were to be invaded. But why did the Germans not use them in the areas of southern England that were so obviously being prepared for D-Day?

It has been suggested that the raid on Grimsby was carried out against orders. Hitler had specifically prohibited further use of the weapon after the first flurry of SD2s dropped on Britain in 1940. He was aware that alerting the Allies to the existence of the weapon could prove counter-productive. A situation report dated 3 June 1943, written for Hitler by Albert Speer (who by 1943 was in charge of industry and armaments in Germany), goes some way towards explaining this strategy: 'Advancement in the development [of weapons] should only be made step by step and only so far as to keep us superior to the enemy. Even if the possibility exists to suddenly make a very great advance, it should be held back in order not to give the enemy the chance to jump the stages of development.'

This strategy may seem to involve a strange kind of logic for the time, but what is known is that by this point in the war the tide was turning and Germany's resources were being stretched to the limit. They were focusing their efforts on the new V series of airborne weapons, which were to prove effective though short-lived (as the next chapter illustrates). But, perhaps most potent of all in the fight in the propaganda war, was the speed, efficiency and bravery which led to Grimsby and Cleethorpes being cleared so quickly. Were it not for Major Parker, Lieutenant Wakeling and the many other men in bomb disposal, perhaps the Nazi war machine would have changed direction and things might have been very, very different.

Lieutenant Wakeling did not leave Grimsby until the end of August 1943. He had dealt with several high explosive bombs and hundreds of butterfly bombs. He did not escape entirely unscathed, being peppered with shrapnel on one occasion. However, he was considered fit enough to be sent to Hull where there was a company that had recently lost a young officer while clearing butterfly bombs. They had put a slab of gun cotton on a bomb and detonated it. The bomb failed to explode but was thrown into the air, ricocheting off two other men and exploding at the feet of the officer. Wakeling took over the young man's section and carried on with his work. The fields of corn were still littered with the little bombs, and tanks were being used to tow the reapers. Understandably farmers were reluctant to drive the harvesters through such a dangerous though vital harvest.

There were to be more casualties in the weeks and months following this raid. It will never be known whether one young boy disturbed a butterfly bomb accidentally or picked it up with the curiosity natural to any child. His headstone stands among others of those who died in the raid with the simple inscription: 'Frank Childs, Aged Nine, Killed by Enemy Action.'

9

Flying bombs and land mines

THE SECOND WORLD WAR saw enormous leaps forward in weaponry and strategy. The increasing use of aircraft for bombing resulted in the unexpected challenges of unexploded bombs. However, bombing raids required manned flight and, as with any operation that required significant levels of trained manpower, it was subject to human error. The Germans knew that to overcome this, the next stage was to master unmanned flight and develop missiles that could cross the Channel to fall on the populous areas of southern England. The Treaty of Versailles drawn up after the First World War was supposed to have prevented Germany from recreating a war machine. However, the Treaty had not been enforced adequately and it was no surprise that among other areas Germany channelled its inventive traditions into the apparently non-military science of rocketry.

Much of the research for V2s was undertaken in Peenemünde, a military testing centre on the Baltic, near the German–Polish border. Allied inspections after the end of the war were to reveal the scale of the development: by then, German science was well advanced, with rockets large enough to be fired upon the United States. Post-war pragmatism soon banished any victorious sense of righteousness and the race was on between the Allies, particularly Russia and the United States, to secure the brains behind these developments. The spoils were shared and scientists were shipped to both countries where they took their places on the starting blocks for the space race – won in 1969 by the United States.

Twenty-five years earlier, in 1944, the precursors of the rockets that were to take man into space were raining down on London and the south-east of England. The V1 and V2 were to take on mythic proportions. The V1 was a flying bomb and generally referred to as the 'doodlebug'. It was characterized by its curious engine sound; those who heard it would wait in dread for the silence that would signal its descent was imminent. The V2 was a long-range rocket that approached almost noiselessly, offering no hope of escape to anything caught in its path.

German intelligence knew of the Allied plans for the invasion of occupied Europe. American troops had flooded into the country, and southern England was being prepared as a base for the gathering invasion force. German strategists planned to use the full force of their V1s and V2s on the troops and embarkation points along the south coast in December 1943. However, British forces were to thwart their plan by launching a peremptory strike against Peenemünde, destroying stocks of V2 rockets in one hit. The night of 17/18 August 1943 – when 571 bombers dropped nearly 2,000 tons of high-explosive and incendiary bombs – is thought to have delayed the ensuing German attack by at least two months. The Luftwaffe was left to launch a desperate echo of previous attacks in a conventional bombing raid on key targets including London, Hull, the east coast and Bristol. It was to be seven months before the first V1 appeared, in the middle of June 1944.

The V1 looked like a small fixed-wing plane powered by a jet engine that sat on top of the fuselage. At nearly 26 feet (8 metres) in length and with a 16-foot (5-metre) wing span, it was capable of carrying 850 kilograms of high explosive. It was operated rather like a child's wind-up aeroplane. A small propeller was governed by a counter, which could be set to a run to a predetermined number of revolutions; thus the distance required to be travelled could be measured. Once the pre-set revolutions were complete, two tiny detonators fired and shifted the craft into a diving position. As the angle changed the fuel supply was cut and the V1 started to travel silently towards the earth. Blast damage was generally substantial.

The V1 was not to be a particular issue for bomb disposal sections, many of which had been reorganized and re-formed ready for invasion. Of the first ten doodlebugs launched against Britain on the night of 12/13 June 1944, five crashed shortly after take-off, one landed in the Channel and four made it to the mainland. All exploded on impact: one on Bethnal Green in east London, one in Sussex and two in Kent. Forty-eight hours later a much larger raid took place when 244 missiles were launched from fifty-five different sites in the Low Countries. It was a terrifying twenty-four hours for people in London and the south-east, but an onslaught on this scale could not be sustained. Nevertheless an average of 155 doodlebugs per day were launched against Britain throughout August.

The fuzing design of the V1 was extremely efficient, but one did land without exploding on 17 June 1944 near Brighton in Sussex. Damage to it was, however, substantial although initial examination revealed two fuzes; plans for immunization were drawn up. Less than a week later a complete V1 was found, again in Sussex; on 24 June, Major John Hudson, who had received the George Medal for his earlier work on the Y fuze, was charged with examining the device, together with Bob Hurst and Dr J. A. T. Dawson from the Ministry of Supply.

They quickly established that the V1 contained three fuzes, the first two of which were the same as those recovered from the earlier incident. The third was rather more mysterious and, being unmarked, presented quite a problem. As was usual in such instances, Hudson was ordered to recover the unknown fuze intact at all costs. It was decided that the best way to proceed was to take a radiograph, which is similar to an X-ray. Unfortunately the mechanism could not be seen clearly and it was impossible to know if there was a booby-trap or anti-withdrawal device lurking underneath.

It was suspected that the fuze contained some kind of timer or clock, and in all likelihood would be set on a short delay. It did not appear to be ticking but, as had been proved on too many occasions, any movement or sudden jarring could prove fatal. This made the proposed plan, to cut a hole in the side of the casing to remove some of the explosive and thus allow cleaner access to the fuze pocket for radiography, a treacherous business. Nevertheless, the operation was undertaken and Hudson and Hurst worked shifts in operating the acid cutting machinery over the five hours required to corrode the metal to the point at which a sharp knife could complete the job.

Once the metal casing had been removed, the filling had to be removed – taking care not to let the acid come into contact with the explosive. Hudson, Hurst and Dawson undertook this difficult job. Acetone was used to wash out the explosive; the toxic fumes induced dizziness and vomiting. After thirteen hours of this very unpleasant and hazardous task, there was enough room to insert the radiographic equipment inside the bomb case to obtain a clear image of the fuze: it was similar to the 17 in operation. There was, however, one difference in that the clockwork section of the fuze could be set only to a maximum of two hours. Fortunately, there was no anti-withdrawal device similar to the Zus40, but it was not possible to determine how long this clock had to run: it could have run its time already, but then again, perhaps there were only seconds to go. Extracting the fuze was not going to be easy.

Recovering the fuze had taken eight days, during which time V1s were dropping out of the sky all around as they were attacked by fighter planes. The explosions were not only disconcerting to those working at the site; they also threatened to cause the clock to start. Yet again, Hudson and Hurst managed to come up with a device that would allow them to remove the fuze remotely while keeping the magnetic clock-stopper close to prevent the clock from starting. As the fuze was drawn out by a system of cords and pulleys, it was pulled into the strong magnetic field created by the clock-stopper. The electric stethoscope was attached and as Hurst listened attentively, while Hudson manipulated the system of ropes, removing the fuze success-fully. Later examination showed it to be fully armed, with only thirty-two minutes to run.

Hudson, Hurst and Dawson had successfully uncovered the secrets of the fuzing mechanism of the V1. On the rare occasion that doodle-bugs did land and not explode, they could be defuzed. However, they usually did explode, to devastating effect. Then the bomb disposal men would search through the debris, looking for new devices that may have been used. On at least one occasion an officer was killed while removing components for examination.

The first V2 rockets arrived in Britain on 8 September 1944. At 45 feet (14 metres) in length and 5 feet (1.5 metres) in diameter, they carried close to one metric tonne of explosive and hit the ground at nearly 5,000 kilometres (3,000 miles) an hour. A particularly terrifying weapon, the first one descended from a very high altitude to explode in Chiswick, west London. The second fell to earth in Epping, 35 kilometres (20 miles) north of London. There was a justifiable fear that this was the beginning of a huge wave of destruction that could engulf the south-east of the country and negate the Allied successes being experienced elsewhere. More than anything, it was hoped that the end of the war was in sight. Morale had to be maintained and it was with this in mind that one officer from bomb disposal was sent to quell fears in Chiswick by telling the inhabitants that a gas main had exploded.

This was not the kind of white lie that could be sustained. Over the next nine months a further 517 V2s were to come crashing to earth over London out of a total of 1,100 that hit the country as a whole. The expected 10 per cent failure ratio of normal bombing raids was slashed, as only four in total failed to explode on impact. Many did, however, fall apart in mid-air, raining down their insides and leaving vital clues to the rockets' operation. As with the doodlebug, the V2 did not become a big problem for bomb disposal. The four that failed to explode – all, as it happened, during March 1945, the last month of the bombardment – fell rather close to one another in rural Essex, so just one officer, Major L. Gerhold, was assigned to deal with them. The rockets aroused a great deal of interest, especially among the Army and a large part of the government. Onlookers turned what was a potentially dangerous bomb site into rather a circus as Major Gerhold directed the successful operation to uncover this rocket whilst excavations continued on the first, which had landed on a farm. With the help of Lieutenant Colonel S. C. Lynn, he cleared the site of unnecessary onlookers. Soon news of another V2 came through and again the curiosity of the various Ministries was aroused. In the midst of this Gerhold proceeded with his work on the third and fourth V2, before returning to the first. For this remarkable work he received the George Medal with Bar.

By the time the last V2 landed on Britain, at the end of March 1945, 8,958 people had been killed and 24,500 seriously injured. In Croydon, just outside London, three-quarters of the houses had been damaged or destroyed.

The V1s and V2s were launched from various sites in the Low Countries, such as the Netherlands and Belgium. Sergeant Cecil Brinton of the Royal Engineers, as we have seen, had carried out many dangerous bomb disposal operations in Britain. In September 1944 he was in the Netherlands, among the first Allied troops to be dropped at Arnhem. The plan was to secure a bridgehead over the Rhine and facilitate an Allied drive into the heart of Germany, but the mission failed. Brinton found himself riding a motorbike in northern Holland heading towards a marshalling yard which, his commanding officer had informed him, contained a train with eight or nine trucks holding the component parts of a V2 rocket. It was suspected to be booby-trapped, and Brinton was to make it safe before it could be moved. The suspicion proved to be correct, and he began what was to be one of the most dangerous undertakings of his career in bomb disposal.

In the first truck and the last truck they had a big 500-kilogram bomb. That's one of the big ones, and in each truck the Germans had placed their demolition charge in metal cases with screw thread so they could attach their igniter with a trip wire. Each truck had a couple of them and they were all connected to an instant fuze.

The loaded trucks contained a knot of trip wires and loose wires so that if any were touched, pulled or released the whole train would explode. Eventually, after hours of patient, calm work, Brinton made the site safe. He was awarded the British Empire Medal for his achievement, and was understandably pleased with his handiwork, as was his commanding officer: 'I went back and he was so pleased with it because if I had made one very slight mistake the whole train would have gone up and there was about two tonnes of explosive in it. It would have blown the whole marshalling yard and probably half the town right off the face of the earth.'

It had not been Brinton's first experience of bomb disposal work abroad – and, as we saw in Chapter 6, skills like his were required in many countries. He had already done a tour in the Middle East, where he had defuzed anti-tank mines. Designed to destroy several tonnes of metal, these were buried in the sand with three wire prongs pointing upwards and attached to the igniter. They were extremely difficult to see, and were set off with a pressure as light as a footstep – throwing up deadly shrapnel. Brinton remembers one particular incident:

A soldier stepped on one of these and it went up, exploded and cut him to pieces and he fell to the ground shouting. He was with a friend, the two of them were always together, and he dashed to try to help him. I shouted out, 'Don't! For Christ's sake!' but I was too late. He stepped on one too and that went up. Killed them both of course.

Land mines do not of course differentiate between friend and foe. It is a deep and tragic irony that of the 490 men who were killed in bomb disposal over the course of the war and first two years of peace, 151 of them were killed clearing British mines from their own coastline. There were 2,000 separate mine fields that needed to be cleared; in 1943 work had begun to clear upwards of 350,000 anti-tank mines. These were 40 pounds (18 kilograms) in weight and had a bow spring in the middle. They were designed to be activated only if something of sufficient weight pressed down on them. Troops should have been able to walk over them safely.

As the threat of invasion had receded and America had entered the war, many of the beach areas were also required for training soldiers for D-Day. Tens of thousands of troops were to be massed in preparation for the single greatest invasion in history. It was vital that they could be adequately prepared as well as having safe areas of beach from which to launch on 6 June 1944. It was not going to be a job that could be completed overnight. In fact it was to take until 1972 for the last minefield to be cleared.

Bomb disposal sections were assigned the job of clearing minefields as bombing had become lighter. The public were becoming vociferous, as Lionel Meynell (who in 1941 had dealt with the 'G' mine) recalls:

It became quite political. Questions were asked in the House of Parliament. People were asking why we still had all these minefields. There were sheep going into them and getting killed, dogs going in, there were children kicking footballs into them and going in and getting killed. People were taking short cuts home. So there was a terrific pressure being brought to bear. There were no bombs coming over so they thought, right, these idle fellas, we'll put them to work!

The German minefields were characteristically ordered, even to the point that the mine keys necessary for arming the mines would all be buried together in one corner of the field. If the clearance teams located the keys, they knew how many mines they had to clear. However, the minefields on the British coasts were not so methodically recorded. In 1940, with Hitler marching through Europe, there had been little time to make adequate maps. John Hannaford, who as we have seen had had his share of hazardous assignments, remembers hearing of the problems.

Nobody knew anything about how to deal with our own mines. What we found was that mines were being laid in a panic.

Theoretically there should have been maps where they were, but the maps were hopeless. In South Wales they were laid in very fine sand so the wind and the tide had turned them over, rusted them, rabbits had got underneath and turned them over. Sometimes they were inches, sometimes they were feet under the surface.

The haphazard way in which the mines were now lying led to another problem: sympathetic detonation. When one mine went off it would set off a whole series of bombs – an entire section could be wiped out if one person made a mistake. Hannaford describes the danger:

It meant that the section who were perhaps a hundred yards away from the action and were perhaps sitting down having a smoke or a sandwich lost their lives through the action of other people. It meant in effect that the work was in many ways turning out more dangerous than the actual disposal of bombs.

Disposing of mines required a particularly disciplined approach if fatalities were to be kept to a minimum. Lionel Meynell, by now a major, was sent to Fishguard in South Wales to take command of 16 Company Bomb Disposal. The casualties experienced in the company had already been high, and Meynell was determined that things would change.

Unfortunately I'd only been there two days when a sergeant and a corporal were both killed clearing mines. I then had a section on the Isle of Wight. Most of these mines had been laid by the Free French and, of course, the maps they kept were pretty incomplete. We knew the area where they were, but we didn't know exactly where they were laid. By now nettles, brambles – sometimes ten feet high – had grown over the minefields, so it was a very difficult operation.

Meynell believed that a rigorous approach was required if things were to change. People were entering the minefields from too many points, not knowing if the area they were approaching had been cleared or not. In addition, the work was carried out in exposed conditions where the senses became quite numb. In the cold and wet it did not take long for hands to be incapable of feeling what they were doing. Meynell needed time to organize: 'I said, "Right. We're going to have the most intensive drill for clearing mines." I asked permission from Western Command for a seven-day stay of activities. This was not particularly well received because of the pressure they were under. However, they did clear it.'

He used the time to institute new procedures. Meynell insisted that any time a minefield was entered it was entered at the same place every time. He had 4-gallon cans painted and placed at the minefield entrance. Although it might have been quicker to go in somewhere else, he made his men go in at the same place every day and worked forward from the marker cans.

I never allowed anyone to stay in the minefield for more than twenty minutes because I reckoned by that time they'd be cold, they'd be miserable, their senses would be numbed and they wouldn't be entirely aware of the job they were doing. I don't think I was popular to start with because I never felt that the level of discipline was as high as it might have been, and this was just another irritation. But I never lost anybody else on the minefields.

John Hannaford's section was not to escape unscathed. In 1943 he and his unit were moved to Narberth in Wales to start clearing mines. It was very early days for mine clearance and the ramifications of anti-tank mines having been left in sand for a couple of years were not fully realized. The salt had rusted through the bow springs and the weight of a child could set them off. Hannaford's time in mine clearance was cut short when he had to leave his section and was sent to London to tutor American troops in bomb disposal in preparation for D-Day. He was distressed to hear of the fate of the men he had come to regard as his friends.

> *I heard that three or four of the men that I had left behind had been killed on the beaches. Somehow it rather touched us. On the one hand, dealing with German bombs, there seemed to be some sort of fairness, if you can use that word. But when it came to losing lives through our own mines it was very hard indeed. Our own mines were the reason for the loss of so many fine young men. That hurts still, it really does.*

Mines were not only buried in sand on the beaches. The seaside piers that before the war had been the locations for fun and jollity were booby-trapped with mines in anticipation of invasion. If the Germans had the idea of arriving in Britain, they would certainly not be allowed access to the Palace or West Pier at Brighton. Captain Ken Revis and his section were given the task of clearing Brighton's famous piers of mines. He had already been responsible for defuzing somewhere in the region of 200 bombs (for which achievement he had been awarded the MBE) when he was sent to the promenade at Brighton.

The only way to get out to the piers was by rowing boat, their connecting platforms having been pulled down as a precautionary measure. Fishermen rowed Revis out to undertake a reconnaissance. He had to get on to the pier from water level by means of a thin rope – far from ideal and requiring a great deal of physical strength.

The mines were lashed to the underside of the boards that made up the floor of the pier. Each one was surreptitiously marked on the board above by a small blue dot of paint. Over the years, the wind and rain of the English south coast had weathered the dots almost into oblivion. After the initial inspection, Revis returned to the West Pier with his corporal. Making the mines safe was a delicate business. He used a small, narrow-bladed saw to lift the planks under which the mines lay: 'I was there with my saw with Corporal Marnock. We were both on our knees and I said to him that it was money for old rope. At that very second the whole thing went up.'

Revis was seriously wounded. The only way off the pier was by bosun's chair over a 115-foot (35-metre) stretch of water. Marnock helped his captain towards it.

I remember shouting, 'Help!' and I could hear the corporal saying, 'Come on, sir.' And he got me to my feet and took me to the gap over the water. I was put on a stretcher and felt myself being carried along the pier. When I got to the turnstiles I heard this girl's voice saying to cover my face up. At that point I shouted out, 'Take the bloody thing off – I'm not dead yet!'

However, Revis was permanently blinded and, much to his regret, had to leave the Army. He went on to have a successful career as a solicitor, and is active in the campaign to reopen the West Pier in Brighton. When he looks back, he regards his time in bomb disposal as being characterized by luck. That luck almost ran out in Brighton, but he is left with a remarkably sanguine outlook on what had happened: 'I didn't think it was particularly odd. I just thought it was what you might call the fog of war. I just took it as part of my job.'

If this book and the series on which it is based had a title which reflected the most common sentiment expressed by those whose stories it seeks to tell, it would be called 'It Was Just a Job'. This phrase was heard so regularly during the interviews with the remarkable men who took part that those of us who listened almost began to believe it. However, it was never long before once again we were hearing of the extraordinary actions of ordinary men.

Many of the men, whose stories are told in this book, would gladly return to this work if they could. That they would, speaks volumes for their honour and courage. No medal could ever shine as brightly as their spirit.

Index